Knitting
BEAUTIFUL BOAS
& SCARVES

Knitting
BEAUTIFUL BOAS
& SCARVES

Ruth Lee

GUILD OF MASTER
CRAFTSMAN PUBLICATIONS

First published 2005 by
GUILD OF MASTER CRAFTSMAN PUBLICATIONS LTD
166 High Street, Lewes
East Sussex BN7 1XU

Text and project design © Ruth Lee 2005

© in the Work Guild of Master Craftsman Publications Ltd

ISBN 1 86108 466 8

British Cataloguing in Publication Data

A catalogue record of this book is available from the British Library.

Managing Editor Gerrie Purcell
Production Manager Hilary MacCallum
Photography Anthony Bailey
Editor Clare Miller
Art Editor Gilda Pacitti
Design Danny McBride

Colour reproduction Wyndeham Graphics
Printed and bound in China by Sino Publishing

Remembering my mum Marjorie whose support and encouragement made this all possible and to my partner Mick Pearce for living through the challenges of yet another deadline; your sense of perspective is invaluable.

Note on Measurements:
Although care has been taken to ensure that imperial measurements are true and accurate, they are only conversions from metric; they have been rounded up or down to the nearest ⅛in, or to the nearest convenient equivalent in cases where the metric measurements themselves are only approximate. When following the projects, use either imperial or metric measurements; do not mix units.

Contents

Introduction

The quiet, meditative process of hand-knitting appeals on many different levels. Rhythmic and repetitive, the making process allows for reflection and provides an opportunity to enjoy the quiet spaces between the noise and bustle of modern-day living. Add to this the desire to own or create something handmade and unique, rather than mass produced, and the current vogue for knitting is easily understood.

As a craft, hand-knitting is accessible, compact and quiet, and can be transported easily, making it a sociable as well as a solitary activity. All that is needed is a minimum of relatively inexpensive equipment and materials along with a little patience, and a real sense of pride and fulfilment arises with the first projects to come off your needles.

On a practical level, the recent revival in the popularity of knitting coincides with the availability of a new generation of modern yarns in tune with contemporary fashion. Appealing across the generations, these new yarns provide a range of inviting, colourful, tactile and lightweight materials that are easy and quick to knit.

The projects in this book include the sophisticated, the practical and the glamorous, and range from easy-to-knit pieces to something a little more challenging for the experienced knitter. The choice is yours.

Materials, Equipment and Knitting Know-how

YARNS

Yarns have their own personalities and can be chosen to reflect a specific mood or concept. In this book each workshop aims to match the sensual qualities of fibres and colours with the project name, thus for Workshop 1 (Relax, page 28) Shimmer 5 and Isis in shades Sahara and Morocco suggested exotic vacations and chill-out holidays in the sun.

For further details about all the yarns turn to the Yarn Index on page 154.

Luxurious to handle, the subtle ever-changing colour palette of **Shimmer 5** from Colinette is easy on the eye and a dream to knit. The reflective properties of this yarn enhance the appearance of the simple, easy-to-knit garter stitch ridge pattern. The softer textures of the spool-knitted tubes in Colinette **Isis** are comfortable and easy to wear.

In complete contrast to Workshop 1, *Relax*, the celebratory mood of Workshop 10, *Carnival* (see page 145), is reflected in the choice of richly contrasting colours of burnt oranges, gold, pink and purple. In *Carnival 1*, the sparkly texture of the gold Lurex **Shimmer** yarn from Rowan contrasts with the wild modern colours of Sirdar **Gigi**.

Knitted in lush, dense yarns with a touch of glitz, the yarns chosen for *Carnival 2* have the added advantage of being lightweight and modern in construction. Here the finished boa makes a big statement complete with added extra cheerleader pompoms reflecting the spirit of carnival but without weighing the wearer down!

Workshop 2, *Allsorts* (see page 42), is a bold, in-your-face statement in modern yarns and colours. Knitted in garter stitch (a more complex stitch pattern would simply be lost in this bold array of contrasting textures) the yarns are deliberately chosen to appear mismatched and clashing, while still working together to create an unexpected harmony.

The trick here is to use a colour or texture as a unifying factor so that the design does not appear to be disjointed. In *Allsorts 1*, for example, a limited colour palette leaning towards the purple, blue, turquoise end of the spectrum marries together the contrasting textures of **Touch of Velvet** (Wendy), Sirdar **Gigi**, Twilley's **Goldfingering** and the lush eyelash qualities of **Intension** from GGH. There are no more than five main

Relax

Carnival

colours, some of which are made up of multiple strands of yarn, but the end result is a wild mix of many different textures and colours, reflecting the spirit of the workshop title *Allsorts*.

In *Allsorts 2*, the soft hairy texture of Sirdar **Gigi** and Stylecraft **Gypsy** is repeated throughout the length of the scarf and in two colours only (lime green and pink) against the backdrop of black and silver sections in Stylecraft **Stardust** and Sirdar **Gigi**.

On a practical level, many of the projects show you how to knit multicoloured fabrics without having to continually change colours. Workshop 7 – *Octopus 1* (see page 110), Workshop 8 – *Reef 1* and *2* (pages 121–131), Workshop 1 – *Relax 2* (page 36), Workshop 9 – *Lagoon 1* and *2* (page 134), and Workshop 4 – *Ripple 1* and *2* (pages 71–79) all utilize a limited number of yarns to optimize colour changes with the minimum of fuss. Yarns such as Noro **Blossom** and **Silk Garden** are a wonder of sophisticated and subtle colour changes as are the whole range of yarns from the Colinette collection and the light reflective hues of the new generation of eyelash yarns such as Wendy **Shimmer** and Elle **Plume**.

Workshop 8, *Reef* (page 121), brings together a range of subtly contrasting textures in close colours. Matt and sheen surface textures contrast with soft feathery yarns that are also chosen for their suitability for the stitch patterns. The small fronds are knitted in a smooth yarn (Wendy **Touch of Velvet**) so as not to lose definition, and also to stand out from the more heavily textured background.

Similarly the clarity of the small all-over eyelet patterns in Workshop 6, *Lattice* (page 94), and Workshop 9, *Lagoon* (page 134), would be overwhelmed if they were knitted in a heavily textured yarn. Texere **Prism** and Texere **Stardust** defined the openwork stitch patterns of Workshop 6 with great clarity, both projects for this workshop being knitted in two closely related colours so as not to break up the regular rhythms of the openwork stitch pattern.

In comparison, the grand eyelets in Workshop 5, *Ice Queen* (page 80), are large enough to be knitted in a spiky eyelash yarn Stylecraft **Icicle** without losing the shape of the pattern, while at the same time adding a new dimension to the finished scarf design.

Yarn Conversions	
UK	**US**
Double knit	Sport
Chunky	Bulky

Octopus

Reef

13

Fibre Content

Choice of yarn fibre is also important in terms of function. For example, viscose is a relatively heavy yarn and makes up a percentage of the fibre content of Colinette **Giotto** and **Enigma** and Texere **Prism**. This particular property made these yarns an ideal choice for Workshop 9, *Lagoon*, and Workshop 6, *Lattice*, since these scarves are meant to drape around the waist and hips as well as the shoulders.

Knitted in a simple garter stitch pattern, in both projects in Workshop 7, *Octopus*, the luxurious feathery and rag yarns speak for themselves. Their soft handle makes them an ideal choice for the long, wavy fronds which are designed to envelop the wearer, moulding themselves to the contours of the body while being appealing, sophisticated and easy to knit. The lush textures of these yarns are lightweight and dense without being heavy to wear, making them a good choice for party-wear. The added advantage is that these yarns are so quick and easy to knit you could be wearing the boa on the same day you started making it!

On the other hand, the more sculptural knitting of Workshop 4, *Ripple* (page 70), as well as the big cables from Workshop 3, *Cocoon* (page 56), need a smooth soft yarn to do full justice to the pattern. On a purely practical level full-bodied wool yarns such as Rowan **Big Wool**, Rowan

Several of the designs, including Reef 1 (see page 121) can be worn around the waist and hips as well as the shoulders, so choose a heavy yarn which drapes well.

Biggy, Sirdar **Bigga** (50% wool and 50% acrylic) are most suited to grand-scale cable design. They can fill out any spaces left by the cable crosses and yet are strong enough to take the strain of this type of cable knitting.

The luxurious handle of Noro **Silk Garden** offers a more subtle interpretation of these relief patterns (Workshop 4, *Ripple 2*) and gives a sense of movement to the ridge patterns with the continually changing shades and hues of soft harmonious colour. This design could equally well have been interpreted in **Wow** or **Bigga** yarn and conversely *Ripple 1* would work in the Noro yarns.

The deep twists and curves of the cable patterns and the undulating surfaces of Workshop 4, *Ripple*, read better when knitted in light colours, or space dyed colours that are relatively close in hue or tone. Darker and more broken colours will obscure these relief-style patterns. The clean lines of these designs would also be lost if knitted in a hairy eyelash type yarn.

With these guidelines in mind, each of the workshop projects can be interpreted to suit individual tastes and sense of occasion. The variations shown for each workshop offer alternative suggestions that will spark off your own ideas for personalized projects.

'Big' yarns, such as Rowan Big Wool and Sirdar Bigga, are ideally suited to chunky cable knits, that have a sculptured texture.

Lattice

Lagoon

TOOLS AND ACCESSORIES

As well as the basic knitting needles, there are a number of small items of equipment that will be useful when making your scarf or boa. Always keep a small pair of scissors and a tape measure to hand while you're working. It's also a good idea to have a notepad nearby to keep a record of your work in progress and jot down new ideas.

Needles

Made in plastic, bamboo or aluminium, needle sizes vary from 2mm to 25mm or even broom-handle size. Thickness counts vary from country to country, and old-size needles are different to new-size metric.

Needle sizes are given in metric throughout this book, with additional US measurements given where available. For additional needle conversions, including those for Old UK, please see the **Needle Size Conversion Table** opposite.

Cable Needles

In cable stitch patterns, selected groups of stitches are transferred from the main body of knitting onto the double-pointed cable needle, and held either to the front or the back of the work on a short double-pointed needle. Cable needles are straight or bent in shape, and should be smaller in size than the main needles.

To make the giant cables featured in Workshop 3, *Cocoon*, you may need to improvise as 15mm size cable needles are tricky to get hold of (try KCG Trading, details on page 156). Possible options include using one end from an old set of 15mm plastic circular knitting needles. Alternatively consider using a double-pointed needle from an interchangeable needle set, usually only available up to 10/12mm, or you could make one from wooden dowelling.

> A needle gauge (see picture on page 18) will help you to double check the size of your needles.

NEEDLE SIZE CONVERSION TABLE		
Metric (mm)	**Old UK**	**US**
2	14	0
2.25	13	1
2.5	–	–
2.75	12	2
3	11	–
3.25	10	3
3.5	–	4
3.75	9	5
4	8	6
4.5	7	7
5	6	8
5.5	5	9
6	4	10
6.5	3	10.5
7	2	10.5/11
7.5	1	10.5/11
8	0	11
9	00	13
10	000	15
12	–	17
15	–	19
20	–	35/36

Circular Knitting Needles

These are designed for knitting seamless items in the round, such as multicolored patterned sweaters, but are also useful for knitting a wide, flat piece of work where a large number of stitches are needed to knit the piece (Workshop 1 for example). They are essentially two short needles connected by a flexible cord. Interchangeable sets of short needles and connecting cords are also available.

Stitch Holder

A large safety pin for storing groups of stitches in waiting.

Row Counter

If you own a knitting machine, use the detachable row counter manually each time you complete a row, or use the barrel-shaped type that can be slid onto the end of a knitting needle.

French Knitting Bobbins

These are wooden or plastic bobbins with four pegs and upwards for making tubular knitting; usually supplied with a bodkin. You can also use a double pointed needle or a fine crochet hook to pull the stitches over the pegs.

Wool Holder

Old-fashioned wool holders made of plastic or Bakelite, with a hole in the top for the yarn to pull through, are another invaluable aid. They keep yarns separate from one another (as in Workshop 9, *Lagoon 2*) and also prevent them rolling on the floor. Make an improvised one from a plastic box or jar with a hole cut in it to pull the yarn through.

Cable needles, needle gauge and stitch holders

Circular knitting needle

Row counters

Pompom sets

Stitch Marker

Coloured plastic loops, and split rings are used for marking rows and/or stitches – say every 10 rows knitted – and particularly when knitting in highly textured yarns where it is difficult to see individual stitches. You can also use small safety pins for this purpose.

Steam Iron and Pressing Cloth

A steam iron will be required for finishing some of the garments. Always check the care instructions on your yarn band before pressing to see which setting to use the iron at. Use the iron with a pressing cloth – choose a cloth made of cotton, as synthetic materials might melt under the heat of a hot iron.

Blocking Board

A foam-backed mat in heatproof material (similar to ironing board covers) marked out in 10cm squares to pin work out for blocking and pressing if required.

Pins

Glass-headed pins for pinning out work on the blocking board.

Sewing Needles

Large-eyed with a blunt end, either in steel or plastic. Smaller eyed for sewing on beads and sequins.

Tie-on Tags

For recording basic information, such as needle size and yarn type, and which can be tied onto samples for future reference.

Pompom Set

Usually made from plastic, this is a set of different sized circles with a hole in the middle for making pompoms (see also below). You can of course make your own from cardboard, or thin plastic cut from an old washing-up liquid or milk bottle.

MAKING A POMPOM

1 Cut out two circles of stout card to the desired size with a smaller hole cut out from the centre. (You can buy a custom-made set of plastic templates in a limited range of sizes, see page 18, bottom right picture).

2 Thread a large-eyed darning needle with a long length of yarn and, holding the two pieces of card or plastic together, wrap the yarn around the cardboard, in and out of the hole until you have covered the circumference of the circle. Bring in new colours and textures as required. Continue wrapping: the thicker the layer of yarn the more dense the pompom.

3 Cut around the circumference between the two circles with a pair of sharp scissors **a**. Take a length of yarn, insert it between the two circles and secure with a firm knot **b**. Remove the circles and trim any loose ends.

3a

3b

KNITTING KNOW-HOW

Put simply, knitting is a series of interlinked loops made by pulling the yarn through each existing loop on a needle to make a new loop, and then discarding the old loop. It is the continued repetition of this process that builds up the length of the work. Once you have mastered this basic process you can vary it to create different patterns and textures.

Knit and Purl

Each stitch (loop) can be worked in such a way that the knots of the stitch come to the front or the back of the work. The latter is referred to as a 'knit' stitch and the former a 'purl' stitch.

All knitting patterns, from the simplest to the most complex, are constructed from these two basic stitches. The most basic knitted fabrics being garter stitch, stocking stitch and ribbing. More complex patterns depend on the juxtaposition of these two stitches one with the other, and might also include increases, decreases, made-stitches and cables.

To make a knit stitch the needle is inserted from the left to the right and the yarn passes around the back of the needle from left to right (see page 23).

A purl stitch is simply the reverse of this process. Here the needle is inserted from the right to the left and the yarn passes around the front of the needle from the right to left (see page 23).

Garter stitch

Stocking stitch

Ribbing

Flat and Circular Knitting

Knitting constructed on pairs of needles is generally worked from left to right in rows, and will produce a flat piece of fabric.

Knitting in the round, also referred to as tubular knitting, is either made on sets of double-pointed needles, or on a circular knitting needle or knitting frame. Each full circle of knitting is called a 'round'.

Determining the Size

The number of individual stitches cast on determines the width of the knitting, while the length is determined by the number of rows. This is still the case even if the knitting is used sideways on (as in Workshop 1, *Relax 2*).

To determine the number of rows and stitches in a piece of knitting, count rows upward from the cast on edge and the stitches horizontally. It is easier to count rows a few stitches in from the outside edge. Due to the highly textured nature of some of the yarns used in these projects, it is a good idea to mark your rows with a plastic split ring, say every six or ten rows, as it is sometimes quite difficult to see individual stitches and rows.

To shape knitting the work can be made narrower or wider at any given point by adding to or subtracting the number of stitches being knitted at any given time.

Tension

Tension (or gauge) refers to the number of rows and stitches to a given measurement and determines the final size of a piece of knitting. This all-important aspect of knitting depends upon the complex interrelationship between needle sizes, thickness of yarn, type of stitch patterns being worked and the tension at which an individual knitter works. This will be the deciding factor as to whether your knitting is the correct size and shape.

Tension is usually expressed as the number of stitches and rows needed to make a 4in (10cm) square of knitting, and can be found on the ball band on the yarn. Generally speaking the lower the number of rows and stitches to 4in (10cm), the thicker the yarn or needles.

Knit a small swatch before starting each project and compare the results with the tensions given. If you find that your swatch is larger than given, try smaller needles. Conversely, if your swatch is smaller, you should change to larger needles. There is obviously a little more leeway with the final measurements of boas and scarves than with garments. Check the overall dimensions of each of the projects on offer, and compare these measurements with your own work.

Knit tension swatches, as described, right, using the needle size suggested in the pattern. Use the tension swatch as a guide to make comparisons. You may feel that a couple of centimetres either way will not be an issue for a scarf or a boa.

HOW TO MAKE A TENSION SWATCH

1 Cast on 20 stitches in the main yarn (see page 22). Knit for 4 rows in main yarn, 2 rows in a contrast colour, and 10 rows in main yarn.

2 Insert a tie marker on the sixth and fifteenth stitch as you knit the next row. Knit a further 10 rows of main yarn, 2 rows of contrast yarn and finally 4 rows of main yarn. Cast off.

3 Using a squared blocking board pin the swatch out so that the edges are parallel to each other. Cover with a cotton cloth and steam press, unless the ball band of the yarn states that you must not do this. If this is the case simply measure as described below.

4 The aim is to work out how many stitches and rows you will need to knit $\frac{1}{3}$in (1cm). Measure the swatch flat between the tie markers first. This will give you a measurement for 10 stitches, for example $1\frac{1}{4}$in (3cm). To find out what $\frac{1}{3}$in (1cm) measures, divide 10 stitches by $1\frac{1}{4}$in (3cm). This will give you a tension of 3.33 stitches to $\frac{1}{3}$in (1cm). From this you can see that 4in (10cm) equals 3.33 multiplied by 10 which is 33 whole stitches.

5 Measure the distance between the top and bottom rows of contrast colours, for example 20 rows equals 2in (5cm). To find out what $\frac{1}{3}$in (1cm) equals in terms of rows, divide 20 rows by 2in (5cm). This will give you a tension of 4 rows to $\frac{1}{3}$in (1cm). From this you can see that 4in (10cm) equals 4 multiplied by 10 which is 40 rows.

6 A 4in (10cm) square is therefore 33 stitches by 40 rows.

MAKING A SLIP KNOT

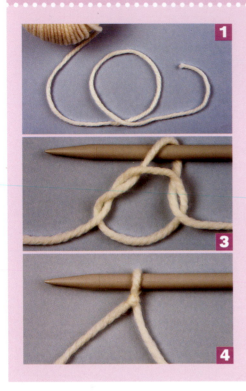

Casting on starts with a slip knot which you make like this:

1 Make a circle of yarn making sure the short end crosses over the long end attached to the ball.

2 Pull the short end through the circle with the point of the needle by inserting the needle so that it is pointing downward, going first under the long end and then over the short end of yarn at the point where both ends cross over each other.

3 Flick the needle upward making a long loop on the stem of the needle.

4 Pull the long end and then the short end of the yarn to tighten the knot.

CASTING ON

1 Measure a length of yarn about three times the measurement of the piece of work to be cast on, and make a slip knot onto the needle at this point. The measured end will be used to cast new loops onto the needle.

2 Hold the needle attached to the ball of yarn in your right hand and the measured length of yarn in your left hand. Keeping the yarn under tension **a**, make a loop around your left thumb and insert the needle under this loop **b**.

3 Wind the yarn from the ball end around the needle from the back to the front. Pull the yarn through the loop on your thumb to make a new stitch **a**, taking the old loop over the needle **b** and dropping it off behind the needle.

4 Close the stitch by pulling the new loop tight before making the next stitch.

KNIT STITCHES

1 Hold the needle with the cast-on stitches in your left hand. With the yarn at the back of the work, and using the right-hand needle, pass the point of this needle up through the first stitch from left to right.

2 Take the yarn from left to right up and over the front of the right needle.

3 With the right-hand needle pull the yarn through the loop on the left-hand needle to make a new stitch on the right-hand needle.

4 Slip the old loop off from the left-hand needle.

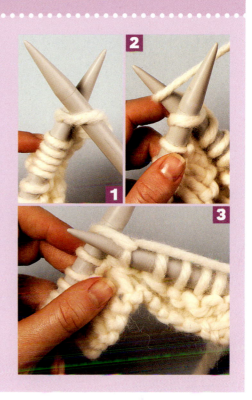

PURL STITCHES

1 Bring the yarn to the front of the work.

2 With the right-hand needle to the front of the left-hand needle, pass the point of the right-hand needle through the loop on the left-hand needle from right to left.

3 Working from right to left, take the yarn around the point of the right-hand needle over the top of the needle to the underneath.

4 Pull the new loop through the stitch on the left-hand needle to make a loop on the right-hand needle and slip the old loop off the left-hand needle.

CASTING OFF KNIT-WISE

1 Knit the first two stitches of the row.

2 Using the left-hand needle, lift the first stitch over the second stitch **a** so that one stitch remains on the right-hand needle **b**.

3 Knit the next stitch and repeat step **2**. Continue in this manner until only one stitch remains on the needle.

4 Break off the yarn and draw the end through the remaining stitch, pulling it tight to close the stitch.

SLIP STITCH

This gives the knitting a neat edge.

1 Insert the right-hand needle into the first stitch on the left-hand needle as if to purl (unless otherwise specified).

2 Without taking the yarn around the needle, pass the stitch over to the right-hand needle.

3 Knit the next and subsequent stitches in the normal way.

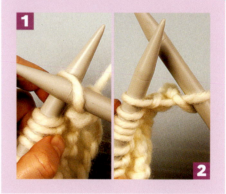

MAKING FRINGES AND TASSELS

1 You will need a cardboard gauge a little longer than the depth of the tassel or fringing. Wrap the yarn around the gauge. Holding the wrappings tightly, cut through one end of the bundle and remove from the template so that the individual ends of yarn remain doubled over.

2 To make a fringe Hook the doubled over yarns through the edge of the knitting with a crochet hook, pass the long ends through the loop and pull tight to knot in place.

3 To make tassels Using either a matching or a contrasting colour yarn, bind the looped end of the bundle of doubled yarns, leaving the tail-ends loose.

Adapting a Pattern

If you decide to make radical alterations to the pattern, such as modifying the stitch pattern, or working with completely different yarns from those suggested in the instructions, you will need to make a tension swatch as described on page 21 to recalculate the correct number of stitches and rows.

To customize an existing design, the easy solution is to source a yarn that will knit up to the tension as given. However as these patterns are for scarves and boas (where the fit is not absolutely critical) a simple way to achieve an approximate measurement is to compare the number of yards (or metres) to, say, $1\frac{3}{4}$oz (50g) of yarn. The greater the lengths of yarn per $1\frac{3}{4}$oz (50g) then the finer the yarn.

For example, $1\frac{3}{4}$oz (50g) of Sirdar **Gigi** is $125\frac{3}{4}$yd (115m) approximately (or $251\frac{1}{2}$yd per $3\frac{1}{2}$oz – 230m per 100g) whilst Sirdar **Bigga** works out at roughly $43\frac{3}{4}$yd per $3\frac{1}{2}$oz (40m per 100g). Sirdar **Bigga** knitted on size 15mm needles gives a tension of 6 stitches and 9 rows per 4in (10cm) square, whereas to knit a 4in (10cm) square in Sirdar **Gigi** on size 4mm needles you will need a tension of 25 stitches and 34 rows.

From this information you can see that these two yarns are not compatible in terms of tension, for example 6 stitches and 9 rows of **Gigi** would only measure approximately $9\frac{1}{2}$ x 10in (2.4 x 2.6cm) whereas 25 stitches and 34 rows of **Bigga** would measure approximately 16 x $14\frac{1}{2}$in (41 x 37cm).

Abbreviations

The earlier patterns in this book are written in long-hand, with later patterns written using standard abbreviations (see right).

ABBREVIATIONS USED IN THIS BOOK

K (or k)	knit
P (or p)	purl
st(s)	stitch(es)
st st	stocking stitch (k1 row, p1 row, rep the 2 rows)
g-st	garter stitch (every row k)
sl	slip
ssk	slip, slip, knit (slip 2 consecutive sts then insert left needle back into the front of the 2 sts and k the two slipped sts together) – i.e. this forms a decrease
psso	pass slip stitch over
lp(s)	loop(s)
tbl	through back loop (i.e. ktbl or k tbl = k next st through back loop)
yf	yarn forward (i.e. yarn to the front)
yb	yarn back (i.e. yarn to the back)
k-wise	knit wise (i.e. as if to k st)
p-wise	purl wise (i.e. as if to p st)
m1	make 1 by picking up thread before next st and K into back of it
inc	increase
dec	decrease
beg	beginning
alt	alternate
foll	following
rnd	round
rep	repeat
patt	pattern
rem	remaining
cont	continue
cm	centimetre(s)
CN	cable needle
L	left
R	right
RS	right side
WS	wrong side
RH	right hand
LH	left hand

The Workshops

Relax

Knitted to be worn together, these long thin scarves can be twisted and intertwined one around the other to create any number of different looks. Featuring contrasting textures and colours, these first patterns are designed for quick and easy knitting worked either on two needles or on a wooden knitting bobbin in all rows knit.

A circular knitting needle is used to accommodate the larger number of stitches needed for this project, and is used in exactly the same way as you would a pair of knitting needles. Bear in mind that when every row is worked as a knit row on two needles, the ridge or knot of the stitch is at the back of the knitting as you work. At the end of each row the knitting is turned, and the next and all subsequent rows are knitted in the same manner.

The resulting fabric (which is traditionally called garter stitch) is firm with ridges on both sides, relatively stable and doesn't curl at the edges. It is these properties that make it a useful stitch for long, straight pieces of knitting, or as an edging for stitch patterns that have a natural curl on the long edges, such as stocking stitch.

Elongated knit stitches (see *Relax 2*, page 36) are made by wrapping the yarn around both needles two or more times, then drawing just one loop through the original stitch (see page 38).

The seamless tube produced on the knitting spool is also worked in all rounds knit. Because the work is not turned at the end of a row, the ridges or knots of the stitch are always at the back of the work, the result being stocking stitch. This is the same as knitting one row and then purling one row on a normal pair of knitting needles.

Stocking stitch tends to curl at the edges when knitted as a flat piece of work and needs edging to make it lie flat. However when this pattern is knitted in rounds this problem no longer exists, as you are making a continuous tube with no outside edges. Again, this makes a suitable stitch pattern for long tubular scarves.

One extra technique needs to be mastered in this first workshop in order to give your work a professional finish. The first stitch of every row is slipped to give a neat edge. This just means that the stitch is slipped from the left needle to the right needle without knitting it. The remainder of the row is knitted as normal.

Relax 1

If you are a beginner, try knitting the two scarves in this part of Workshop One first. You will only need to cast on a small number of stitches (see page 22), then simply knit back and forth (or round and round) until you reach the required length for your scarf.

Materials
- 1 x 3 ½ oz (100g) hank each **Colinette Shimmer 5** in shade **A** – Sahara (135) and **B** – Morocco (127)
- 1 x 3 ½ oz (100g) hank each of **Colinette Isis** in shade **C** – Sahara (135) and **D** – Morocco (127)

Equipment
- 1 pair 12mm needles (US 17)
- 1 four-prong knitting spool
- 1 double-pointed needle

Techniques
- Cast on and off
- Knit stitch
- Slip stitch
- Bobbin knitting

Narrow Garter Stitch Scarves

1 Using 12mm (US 17) needles and **A** cast on 5 stitches with one needle and two ends of yarn.

2 SL1, K4. This instruction is asking you to slip 1 stitch and then knit 4 stitches. See pictures **a** **b** and **c**.

3 Repeat step **2** until yarn runs out. The strips shown on page 30 measure approximately 98½in (250cm). Cast off.

4 Make a second piece the same in **B**.

Knitted tubes

1 Using a four-prong spool, cast on 4 stitches in **C**. To do this you first pull the end of yarn down the centre of the bobbin and then continue to wrap the yarn loosely around each of the four pegs, from back to front and around the peg.

2 Bring the yarn from the back of the last wrapped peg to the front of the first wrapped peg **a**. Holding the bobbin in your left hand and the pick (a double-pointed knitting needle for example) in your right hand pull the bottom loop of yarn over the top row of yarn **b**. Pull the loose end of the yarn downwards to secure this first stitch.

3 Continue in this manner, wrapping the working yarn around the front of the pegs and knitting off each individual stitch as described in step **2**, until the tube is the required length.

4 Cast off thus. Place the working end of yarn behind the next peg to be knitted, then transfer the last stitch you have knitted to this peg **a**. Bring the lower loop on the peg over the upper loop **b**. Pull the knitteing down tight and continue in this manner until 1 stitch remains.

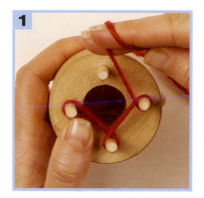

5 Cut the yarn leaving a long end to pull through the remaining loop.

6 Make a second piece the same in colour **D**.

Relax 1 variations

▶ Tubular stripes

This sample uses horizontal, vertical and spiral stripes. To knit the horizontal stripes, work on a four-prong spool, knitting one full round first in the light colour followed by the same in the darker colours (Rowan **Biggy Print** and Noro **Blossom**). The yarn not being knitted is carried on the inside of the bobbin and then exchanged with the working colour at the end of each round. The colour sequence here would be 2 light-coloured stitches followed by 2 dark-coloured stitches and finally 2 light-coloured stitches.

To knit vertical stripes, work with alternating colours on a four-pronged spool so that the light colour stitch is always knitted off with light colour yarn and the dark stitch is knitted off with the dark coloured yarn.

◀ Blended colours

Tubes knitted in several ends of yarn plied together to give a subtle range of graduated colours, which relate to each other by way of a common colour story. To do this, try combining the same yarn with alternative colours for each new version of the tube. The low key graduated shades in the Noro range (**Blossom** or **Secret Garden**) work well here plied with a black glitter and viscose yarn. The thicker of the tubes carries the same shade of Noro yarn as the thinner tube, but here it is plied with a second strand of Noro in a different colour range.

▶ Matching garter stitch stripes

A selection of narrow garter stitch strips knitted to complement the colours and textures of the tubes shown in sample 2. The black glitter and viscose yarn is used to link the colours together.

◀ Various yarns plied together

A wider strip of garter stitch knitting worked in 2 ends of Noro yarn plied with black viscose and glitter, designed to be worn on its own or with one or more of the examples from samples 2 and 3.

Relax 2

Relax 2 extends the possibilities of working with all rows knit by introducing you to sideways knitting in elongated garter stitch on a circular knitting needle (see below). Here you are casting on a large number of stitches, but knitting only a very few rows to complete the work. The long length of the scarf relates to the number of stitches cast on, and the shorter width equates to the number of rows knitted.

Materials
- 1 x 3½ oz (100g) hank **Giotto** by Colinette Yarns in Shade **A** – Sahara (135)
- 1 x 3½ oz (100g) hank **Isis** by Colinette Yarns in Shade **B** – Sahara (135)

Equipment
- 1 circular knitting needle size 7mm (US 10.5/11)

Techniques
- Cast on and off
- Knit stitch
- Elongated knit stitch
- Slip
- Working with a circular needle

1 Cast on 160 stitches in **A**.

2 K3 rows **A**.

3 Change to **B**, K2 rows. **a b**

3a

3b

Knitting note
Do not break the yarn off at the end of rows unless instructed to do this.

5a

5b

5c

4 Change back to **A**, K 3 rows.

5 K 1 row elongated stitch using a double throw to make the elongated stitch. **a** **b** **c**

6 K 1 row in **A** and break off yarn.

7 Change to colour **B**, K 1 row.

8 Rejoin colour **A**. K 1 row.

9 As step 5.

10 As step 2.

11 As step 3.

12 As step 2.

13 Cast off all stitches evenly.

14 Stitch in loose ends.

15 Make tassels in **A** and **B** (see page 24)

16 Attach tassels to short ends of scarf.

Tassels are simple to make (see page 24 for instructions) and on the right scarf will provide a finished look without being stiff and formal.

Relax 2 variations

▶ Broken & solid stripes

Vary the look of garter-stitch stripe patterns by exchanging colours on either all the even number rows, or on first an odd number row followed by an even numbered row. The latter will result in a mix of solid and broken stripes. If the knot of the stitch is on the back of the knitting then the right side of the stripe will have a solid edge. However if the knot of the stitch is front facing, the edge of the stripe will appear to be broken. These three small swatches knitted over 10 stitches exchange colours and yarn types at different intervals on first even, and then odd, number rows and as a mix of the two. The amount of rows knitted for each stripe varies between two, three, four and five rows.

◀ Even number of row stripes

In this example, which is knitted over 24 stitches on 7mm needles, there are an even number of rows per stripe thus: knit 2 rows **A** normal length knit stitch and 1 row **B** normal length and 1 row as an elongated knit stitch. These four rows are repeated three times. Knit 2 more rows in **A** and cast off loosely.

▶ Odd and even numbers of rows

Odd and even numbered rows form this stripe pattern of 5 rows normal length knit stitch in **A**, followed by 2 rows of **B**. The second row of the latter is knitted as an elongated stitch. Repeat this sequence twice and finish on 5 more rows of **A** before casting off

◀ Openwork stripes

Here, the elongated knit stitches are worked in **A** and the normal length knit stitch in **B**. To knit a similar pattern, knit 3 rows in **B**, change to colour **A** and knit 1 row normal knit stitch, 1 row elongated and 1 row normal length, change to colour **B** and knit 2 rows. Repeat this sequence twice and cast off.

Allsorts

Colourful scarves in an anarchic mix of contrasting textures are knitted using the short row or partial knitting technique. This creates wedge-shaped sections of flat, interlinked surface pattern in solid colours and stripe patterns.

The same technique can be manipulated to create three-dimensional shapes and forms (see Workshop 4, *Ripple*) but here the emphasis is on two-dimensional geometric patterns, knitted in garter stitch only for *Allsorts* 1, and in a mix of stocking stitch and garter stitch for *Allsorts* 2.

The first project is knitted sideways-on (lots of stitches and a few rows) where the long, thin rectangular shape of the scarf is sub-divided into two wedge shaped sections, each of which is knitted in stripes of contrasting colours and textures. The striped wedges of pattern are divided by a diagonal stripe running from the top left corner to bottom right corner of the scarf. Each of the wedges is knitted independently from the other, but interlinked in a simple-to-follow version of the short row technique.

The second project (page 50), which is more complex to knit, is made up of a mix of solid colour wedges and stripe sections that are repeated throughout the length of the scarf. Strong, contrasting colours are used for maximum impact of this technique.

To avoid a hole at the point where the knitting is turned, you will need to wrap the next stitch before turning the work. If the last stitch worked was a knit stitch, slip the next stitch from the left needle purl-wise to the right needle, bring the yarn from the other side of the work and return the slipped stitch to the left needle. Turn the work, returning the yarn to the back of the work if the next stitch is a knit stitch, or leaving yarn forward if the next stitch is a purl stitch.

Allsorts 1

The first project is knitted sideways-on (lots of stitches and a few rows) where the long, thin rectangular shape of the scarf is subdivided into two wedge-shaped sections, each of which is knitted in stripes of contrasting colours and textures. The striped wedges of pattern are divided by a diagonal stripe running from the top left corner to bottom right corner of the scarf. Each of the wedges is knitted independently from the other, but interlinked in a simple-to-follow version of the short row knitting technique.

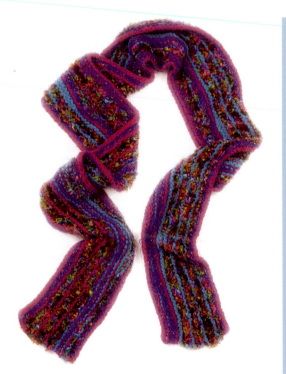

This scarf is approximately 94½in (240cm) long and 5½in (14cm) wide.

Materials

- 2 x 1¾oz (50g) balls each of Wendy **Velvet Touch** in shade **A** – 2052 (Plum), **Intension** by GGH in shade **D** – 05, and Wendy **Velvet Touch** in shade **E** – 2054 (Rich Turquoise)
- 1 x 1¾oz (50g) ball of **B** – Sirdar **Gigi** in shade 051 (Electrique Blue)
- 1 x 1oz (25g) ball of **C** – Twilley's **Goldfingering** in shade WG 62

Equipment

- Size 6mm (US 10) circular knitting needle
- Plastic split ring row markers

Techniques

- Cast on and off
- Knit
- Short row knitting
- Wrap and turn
- Knitting with multi colours

Knitting Notes

When working on circular needles and a number of different colours, it is a good idea to put a marker at the beginning of the first row so that you know which end is the starting point.

Use a marker when knitting a series of short rows on a large number of stitches to denote how many stitches were knitted on the previous short row. This saves you having to count stitches along the whole of the row on the next short row.

1 Measure a length of yarn 2.5 times the approximate length of the finished scarf; in this case 5¾yd (5m).

2 Using a 6mm (US10) circular needle cast on 250 stitches in **A** using the one needle and 2 ends of yarns. K 1 row. Leave **A** attached.

3 Change to **B** plus **C** and K 2 rows. Break off these two colours.

4 Short row knitting commences here. The colour sequence is 2 rows **A** followed by 4 rows of **D** and commences with **A** and ends on **C**. The short row knitting sequence is as follows. Knit 225 stitches and turn and knit back on these 225 stitches **a** **b** **c** **d** **e**. Knit 200 stitches and turn and knit back on these 200 stitches. Continue, decreasing the number of stitches by a factor of 25 on every alternative row until all stitches have been knitted in this manner.

5 Knit all stitches as follows. 1 row in **E** followed by 2 rows each in **B** plus **C**, **A** and **E**. You should now be at the opposite side of the knitting to start work on the second wedge shape.

6 Short row knitting commences here. The colour sequence is 2 rows **B** plus **C** followed by 4 rows of **E** commencing with **B** plus **C** and ending on **E**. The short row knitting sequence is as follows. Knit 25 stitches and turn and knit back on these 25 stitches. Knit 50 stitches and turn and knit back on these 50 stitches. Continue, increasing the number of stitches by a factor of 25 on every alternative row until all stitches have been knitted in this manner.

7 K 2 rows **D** and 1 row **A**. Cast off with a loose even tension.

Allsorts 1 variations

▶ Contrasting textures

Knitted on size 6mm needles over 30 stitches in all rows knit, this sample is knitted in alternate pairs of rows in colours **A** (shade 04 **Intension** from GGH) and **B** (which comprises 4 ends of **Goldfingering**). The latter made up of 2 ends of emerald green (shade 34) and 2 ends of turquoise (shade 53). Short row knitting is in increments of 5 stitches on alternate rows. The diagonal stripe across all stitches is in **Goldfingering**.

◀ Contrasting textures & colours

Here the colour balance is changed, with an emphasis on sparkly, light reflecting blues (Twilley's **Goldfingering** and Elle **Plume**) contrasting with highly textured broken stripes in a wispy burnt orange colour (**Gypsy** from Stylecraft, shade 5118 Mystic).

▶ Wispy stripes & glitz combined

In this example the design is worked in a combination of the blue green **Goldfingering** from samples 1 and 2 combined with broader stripes of **Gypsy** (sample 3) working with the same short row knitting sequence.

◀ Stocking stitch variation

Knitted in the same colour combination as sample 2, this example is worked in stocking stitch (1 row knit followed by 1 row purl) using the same short row knitting sequence as samples 1 – 3.

Allsorts 2

The second project, which is more complex to knit, is made up of a mix of solid colour wedges and stripe sections that are repeated throughout the length of the scarf. Strong, contrasting colours are used for maximum impact of this technique.

Materials
- 2 X 1¾oz (50g) balls of **A** – Stylecraft **Gypsy** Shade 5114 Pink
- 1 X 1¾oz (50g) ball of **B1** – Stylecraft **Stardust DK** shade black/silver and **B2** – Sirdar **Gigi** shade 046 Etoile Black
- 2 X 1¾oz (50g) balls **C** – Sirdar **Gigi** shade 043 Citron Lime

Equipment
- One pair 6mm needles (US 10)

Techniques
- Cast on and off
- Knit
- Purl
- Short row knitting
- Wrap and turn

Tension
- Measured over stocking stitch (colours **A** and **C**) 10cm is 16 sts and 22 rows.

- Measured over garter stitch (colour **B**) 10cm is 14 stitches and 22 rows.

Knitting Notes

Colour **A** used double throughout.

Colour **B** 1 strand Stylecraft Stardust combined with 1 strand Sirdar Gigi.

Colour **C** used double throughout.

The 2 stitches on the left and right edges are always worked as knit stitches and the first stitch of each row is slipped

1 Cast on 14 stitches in colour **B**, K 4 rows garter stitch.

2 * Colour **B**, K 4 rows garter stitch, colour **A**, K 2 rows stocking stitch *. Colour **B**, K 4 rows garter stitch, colour **C**, K 2 rows stocking stitch. Repeat from * to * once more.

3 Short row knitting technique. Join in colour **C** and K 1 row all stitches. Working in stocking stitch and commencing with a purl row, purl 12 stitches and turn. Knit back on these 12 stitches. Colour **B**. Purl 10 stitches and turn. Knit back on these 10 stitches. Colour **C**. Purl 8 stitches and turn. Knit back on these 8 stitches. Colour **B**. Purl 6 stitches and turn. Knit back on these 6 stitches. Colour **C**. Purl 4

stitches and turn. Knit back on these 4 stitches. Colour **B**. Purl 2 stitches and turn. Knit back on these 2 stitches. Colour **C**. Purl all stitches. **a b c d e f g**

4 Colour **B**. Knit in garter stitch for 3 rows over all 14 stitches.

5 Short row knitting technique. Join in colour **A** and purl 1 row all stitches. Working in stocking stitch and commencing with a knit row, knit 2 stitches and turn. Purl back on these 2 stitches. Knit 4 stitches and turn. Purl back on these 4 stitches. Knit 6 stitches and turn. Purl back on these 6 stitches. Knit 8 stitches and turn. Purl back on these 8 stitches. Knit 10 stitches and turn. Purl back on

these 10 stitches. Knit 12 stitches and turn. Purl back on these 12 stitches. Knit 14 stitches. **a b c d e**

6 Colour **B**. K 2 rows. Colour **A**. P 1 row, K 1 row. Colour **B**. K 2 rows. Colour **C**. P 1 row, K 1 row. Colour **B**. K 2 rows.

7 Repeat steps **2** to **6** only this time at step **3** the knit and purl rows are reversed; that is, step **3** commences with a purl row and ends on a knit row and step **5** commences on a knit row and ends on a purl row.

8 Colour **B**, K 4 rows garter stitch, colour **C**, K 2 rows stocking stitch, colour **B**, K 4 rows garter stitch, colour **A**, K 2 rows stocking stitch. Colour

B, K 4 rows garter stitch, colour **C**, K 2 rows stocking stitch.

9 Repeat step **2**.

10 Repeat steps **2** to **9** four times in all. Cast off all stitches. Neaten loose ends.

3g

5a

5b

5c

5d

5e

Allsorts 2 variations

▶ Idea for a border pattern

Knitted in much the same way as the main boa pattern, except that the wedge colours are worked in a different order. Try this version as a border pattern where the main length of the boa is knitted in black with narrow bands of contrasting lime green or pink knitted at irregular intervals.

◀ Short row knitting with curved outside edge

To create the curved edge, the multi-coloured stocking-stitch wedges all commence from the same side of the knitting, and are divided by an even number of garter stitch rows. In this example 6 rows have been knitted in black.

Each wedge shape is knitted in the same manner thus: knit 2 rows on all 14 stitches. Commence short row knitting as follows: decrease 2 stitches on every other row i.e. knit 2 rows on 12 stitches, 2 rows on 10 stitches, 2 rows on 8 stitches. Work in this manner until all stitches have been knitted. Knit 2 rows on all 14 stitches.

▶ Black with thin bright stripes

Knitted mainly in garter stitch, the dominant colour is black with narrow slices of bright colours. The latter are knitted in a mix of stocking stitch and garter stitch for a more random look than the original boa pattern.

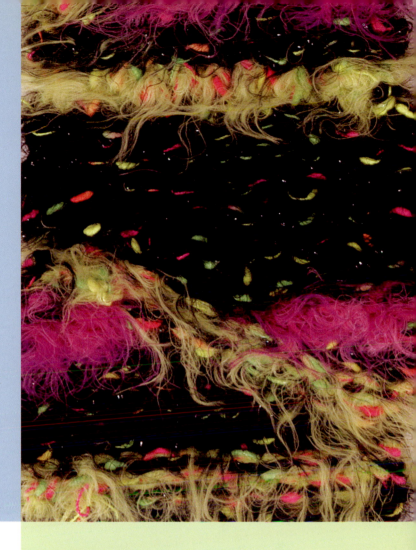

◀ Short row knitting with wavy outside edges

In the final example, working the same type of wedge shape on first one side and then on the other makes the wavy edge of the knitting. *To do this knit 2 rows on all 14 stitches. Commence short row knitting as follows: decrease 1 stitch only on every other row i.e. knit 2 rows on 13 stitches, 2 rows on 11 stitches, 2 rows on 10 stitches. Work in this manner until all stitches have been knitted. *

Each wedge shape is divided by 3 rows of garter stitch in black. If you intend to vary the pattern you need to work an odd number of rows so that the next wedge shape is commenced at the opposite edge of the knitting.

Repeat from * to * to knit the next wedge section, followed by 3 rows of garter stitch.

Cocoon

Cable patterns are formed by crossing groups of stitches one over the other. Stitches are transferred from the main body of knitting onto the double-pointed cable needle, and held either to the front or the back of the work. If the stitches are to cross to the left, they are held at the front of the knitting and to the back for a right cross. These crossings are repeated at regular intervals; every 6th, 8th or 10th row depending upon the pattern.

You will need a short double-pointed cable needle either equivalent in size, or slightly smaller than, the main needle size.

You might like to knit a practice sample in a simple single cable stitch pattern before knitting your first cable stitch project. Cast on 12 stitches and knit 2 rows garter stitch. *Row 3: purl 3, knit 6 and purl 3 stitches. Row 4: knit 3, purl 6 and knit 3 stitches *. Repeat from * to * 3 times. Row 7: purl 3, slip 3 stitches onto the cable needle and place at front of work, knit the next 3 stitches and then knit the 3 stitches from the cable needle. Purl 3 stitches. Row 8: as row 4.

Repeat these 8 rows, except that every alternate cable crossing is worked thus: purl 3, slip 3 stitches onto the cable needle and place at back of work, knit the next 3 stitches and then knit the 3 stitches from the cable needle. Purl 3 stitches.

Cocoon 1

To work the cable crosses successfully, knit the stitches off from the cable needle in the same order they were taken from the main needle. When knitting the cables hold the cable needle parallel to the latter while taking care not to lose stitches off the end of the cable needle.

Knitting Note

Note that the first cable crossing is knitted differently from all other cable crosses to make a symmetrical beginning and ending to the scarf.

Materials

• 3 X 3½oz (100g) balls of Sirdar **Bigga** yarn, shade 688 Delta Blue (1 X 3½oz (100g) ball will knit approximately 7 repeats of the cable pattern).

Equipment

• 1 pair plastic 15mm (US 19) needles
• 1 cable needle of equivalent size or slightly smaller.

Techniques

• Cast on and off
• Knit
• Purl
• Front and back cable crosses

1 Using 15mm (US 19) needles cast on 12 stitches.

2 K 2 rows in garter stitch.

3 K 6 rows in stocking stitch.

4 First cable crossing: slip first 3 stitches onto cable needle and hold to front of work **a**, knit next 3 stitches **b**, knit the 3 stitches from cable needle **c**, slip next 3 stitches onto cable needle and hold to back of work, knit next three stitches **d**, knit 3 stitches from cable needle **e**.

4a

5 Repeat step **2**.

6 Repeat step **3**.

7 Second and all subsequent cable crossings: slip first 3 stitches onto cable needle and hold to back of work, knit next 3 stitches **a**, knit the 3 stitches from cable needle, slip next 3 stitches onto cable needle and hold to front of work, knit next three stitches. Knit 3 stitches from cable needle **b**.

8 Repeat steps **5**, **6**, and **7**, 20 times in all ending with step **7**.

9 Repeat steps **6**, **7** and **8**, 20 times in all ending with step **8**.

10 Knit 3 rows in stocking stitch.

11 K2 rows garter stitch.

12 Cast off.

7a

7b

Cocoon 1 variations

▶ Symmetrical cables

This example is knitted over 12 stitches, the cable crossings are 8 stitches wide and the 2 left and right edge stitches are knitted straight throughout, slipping the first stitch of every row to give a neat edge. To make the cable crossing: knit 2 stitches, slip next 2 stitches onto cable needle and hold to back of work and knit the next 2 stitches. Knit the 2 stitches from cable needle, slip next 2 stitches onto cable needle and hold to front of work, knit next two stitches. Knit the 2 stitches from cable needle. Knit 2 stitches. Purl the next row keeping edge stitches as knit stitches.

◀ Big cable plait

A big cable pattern similar to the main pattern but knitted over 13 stitches. To make the cable crossing: slip first 3 stitches onto cable needle and hold to back of work and knit next 3 stitches. Knit the 3 stitches from cable needle, knit 1 stitch, slip next 3 stitches onto cable needle and hold to front of work. Knit next 3 stitches and then the 3 stitches from cable needle. Purl the next row.

▶ Off-set cables

Cable plait pattern repeat is 12 stitches and 8 rows. Knit 4 rows in stocking stitch. To make first cable crossing slip first 4 stitches onto cable needle, hold to back of work and knit next 4 stitches. Knit the 4 stitches from cable needle. Knit remaining 4 stitches. Purl next row. To make second cable crossing, knit first 4 stitches, slip next 4 stitches onto cable needle and hold to front of work. Knit next 4 stitches and knit the 4 stitches from cable needle. Purl next row. These 8 rows form the pattern, repeat as required.

◀ Cable plait with garter stitch border

Cable plait with garter stitch border the pattern repeat is 16 stitches and 8 rows knitted as sample 3. The garter stitch border is 2 stitches wide at left and right edges.

Cocoon 2

To make the cable stand out, choose a smooth yarn with plenty of body in a light to medium shade and surround the cable with a purl facing stitch or a border of garter stitch.

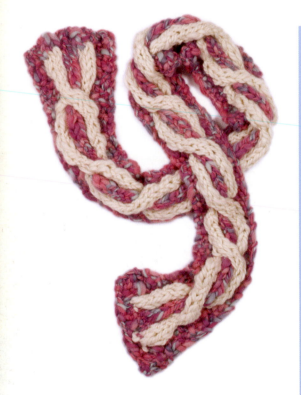

This scarf is approximately 82½in (210cm) long and 8in (20cm) wide.

Materials
- 3 x 3½oz (100g) balls of **A** – Rowan **Biggy Print Wool**, Giddy (239)
- 2 x 3½oz (100g) balls of **B** – Rowan **Biggy Print Wool**, Sheep (258)

Equipment
- 1 pair plastic size 20mm (US 35/36) needles
- 1 cable needle slightly smaller in size than the main knitting needles

Techniques
- Cast on and off
- Knit
- Purl
- Front and back cable crosses
- Knitting cables in two colours
- Moss stitch

Tension
- 5.5 sts and 7 rows to 4in (10cm) measured over stocking stitch.

Knitting Notes

Bicoloured cables knitted in soft, easy-to-knit big yarns from Rowan show you how to develop further the cable technique explored in *Cocoon 1*. The colours not in knit at any given time are stranded across the back of the work in the same manner as two-coloured Jacquards. This only happens at the back of the cable crosses and not the edge stitches.

The 3 edge stitches at left and right are knitted as moss stitch throughout: K1, P1, K1 except the first stitch of each row which is slipped throughout.

When knitting these multi-coloured stripe and cable patterns make sure that you always knit the same group of stitches in the same colour throughout.

1 Using 20mm (US 35/36) plastic needles cast on 15 stitches in **A**.

2 * K1 P1* **a** **b** **c** until 1 stitch remains, K1. Knit a second row in the same manner.

3 Commence knitting in two colours thus: 3sts **A**, 3 sts **B**, 3sts **A**, 3 sts **B**, 3 sts **A**. The colour that is not knitting is stranded across the back of the work.

4 Knit 8 rows of stocking stitch, excepting the 3 left and right edge stitches that are knitted as moss stitch.

5 Cable row: front cross keeping to the colour sequence as outlined above **a**. K1, P1, K1, make the cable crossing thus: slip first 6 stitches onto cable needle **b**, hold to front of work and knit next 3 stitches. Now slip 3 sts from the left-hand end of the cable needle back onto the left knitting needle and knit these sts in the correct order, finally knit the 3 remaining sts from the cable needle and K1, P1, K1 **c** **d** **e** **f** **g**.

6 Purl next row except edge stitches which are moss stitch.

7 Repeat steps **4** to **6** inclusive 13 times in all and then step **4** once more.

8 Break off **B** and continue to knit in **A**. Repeat step **2**. Cast off.

Cocoon 2 variations

▶ Criss-cross cable on light background

Knitted on size 12mm (US 17) needles in shade 001 (White Hot) and 022 (Swish) these big cables are knitted as for the main boa, except that every other cable is a back crossing. To do this K1, P1, K1, make the cable crossing thus: slip first 6 stitches onto cable needle, hold to back of work and knit next 3 stitches. Now slip 3 sts from the left-hand end of the cable needle back onto the left knitting needle and knit these sts in the correct order, finally knit the 3 remaining sts from the cable needle and K1, P1, K1.

◀ Three colour criss-cross cable

In this example only 6 rows are knitted between each cable crossing and each block of cables is divided by 4 rows of moss stitch. Colours are Lucky 020, Swish 022 and White Hot 001.

► Criss-cross cable with moss stitch border

Knitted in shades White Hot 001 and Whoosh 014 the cable section is worked over 11 stitches and subdivided thus: 3 stitches shade 001, 5 stitches shade 014 and 3 stitches shade 001. As before the left and right borders comprise 3 stitches knitted in moss stitch throughout and there are 10 rows between each cable crossing. Work the cable row thus: K1, P1, K1, to make the cable crossing slip the first 8 stitches onto a cable needle, hold to front of work and knit next 3 stitches (shade 001). Now slip 5 sts (shade 014) from the left-hand end of the cable needle back onto the left knitting needle and knit these sts in the correct order, finally knit the 3 remaining sts (shade 001) from the cable needle and K1, P1, K1.

The sample shows three repeats of the cable pattern: first as a front cable cross, and then three repeats as a back cross.

◄ Criss-cross cable on dark background

A narrow sample knitted over 11 stitches, where the cable section is worked over the centre 5 stitches subdivided thus: 2 stitches left of centre, just 1 central stitch and 2 stitches right of centre. As before, the left and right borders comprise 3 stitches knitted in moss stitch throughout, and there are 6 rows between each cable crossing. Work the cable row thus: K1, P1, K1, to make the cable crossing slip the first 3 stitches onto a cable needle, hold to front of work and knit next 2 stitches (shade 001). Now slip 3 sts (shade 021) from the left-hand end of the cable needle back onto the left knitting needle and knit these sts in the correct order, finally knit the 2 remaining sts (shade 001) from the cable needle and K1, P1, K1.

Ripple

Short row knitting techniques are exploited in this workshop to create big, sculptural braids in Sirdar Wow (a soft 100% polyester chenille yarn), or softer ridges knitted in Noro Silk Garden. The pintuck ridge in Ripple 2 is simply a closed version of the open ripple detailed in Ripple 1.

Try a practice sample for wavy ripples and the knitted-in pintuck. Cast on 20 stitches. Knit 2 rows garter stitch and 10 rows in stocking stitch. Working in stocking stitch, knit 16 stitches and turn and purl back. * Knit 12 stitches and turn and purl back. Knit 8 rows of stocking stitch on these 12 stitches only ending with a purl row *. Knit these 12 stitches and the 4 edge stitches. Purl back 20 stitches. Knit 10 rows. Repeat from * to *.

To make the pintuck, use a spare needle (smaller in dimensions than the main needles) and pick up 12 loops from the first row of the pintuck section. The point of the spare needle should be facing in the same direction as the main needle.

The aim is then to knit off a stitch from the spare needle, and the equivalent stitch from the main needle in one operation.

Ripple 1

Knitted in a soft, full-bodied yarn for maximum sculptural effect. The centre group of five stitches are knitted over more rows than those on the outside edge to create the wavy ripple.

1 Cast on 11 sts with 7mm (US 10.5/11) needles and K1 row.

2 K8 rows stocking stitch (st st).

3 K3 edge sts, K5 more sts and turn the knitting.

4 Purl (P) 5 sts and turn.

5 K8 rows st st on these 5 sts beginning with a knit row and ending with a purl row. Turn the knitting: **a** **b**.

6 K5 sts and then the 3 edge sts.

7 K3 sts, P5 sts and K3 sts.

8 Repeat steps **2** to **7**, 28 times in all.

9 Repeat step **1**.

10 K2 rows garter st (g st).

11 Cast off all sts.

12 Neaten all ends.

Materials
- 3 x 3½oz (100g) balls of Sirdar **Wow** in Blue Ice (751)

Equipment
- 1 pair 7mm (US 10.5/11) needles

Techniques
- Cast on and off
- Knit
- Purl
- Short row knitting

Tension
- 15 rows and 8 stitches to 4in (10cm).

Ripple 1 variations

▶ Offset ripples

Offset ripples. Cast on 11 stitches and knit 2 rows garter stitch. Change to stocking stitch. Knit 9 stitches and turn the knitting. Purl 5 stitches and turn. Knit 10 rows on these 5 stitches only ending on a purl row. Knit these 5 stitches and the remaining 2 stitches. Purl all 11 stitches. Knit 1 row. Purl 1 row. Knit 7 stitches and turn the knitting. Purl 5 stitches and turn. Knit 10 rows on these 5 stitches only ending on a purl row. Knit these 5 stitches and the remaining 4 stitches. Purl all 11 stitches. Knit 1 row. Purl 1 row.

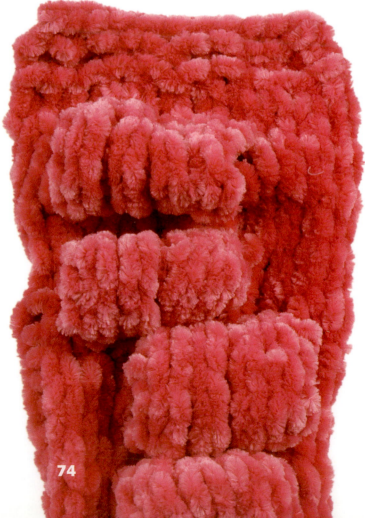

◀ Pairs of offset ripples

Offset ripples in alternating pairs. Cast on 11 stitches and knit 2 rows garter stitch. Change to stocking stitch. * Knit 9 stitches and turn the knitting. Purl 5 stitches and turn. Knit 10 rows on these 5 stitches only ending on a purl row. Knit these 5 stitches and the remaining 2 stitches. Purl all 11 stitches. Knit 1 row. Purl 1 row *. Repeat from * to * twice. ** Knit 7 stitches and turn the knitting. Purl 5 stitches and turn. Knit 10 rows on these 5 stitches only ending on a purl row. Knit these 5 stitches and the remaining 4 stitches. Purl all 11 stitches. Knit 1 row. Purl 1 row **. Repeat from ** to ** twice.

▶ Wavy slits

Wavy slits. Cast on 26 stitches and knit 3 rows in garter stitch. * Knitting as for short row knitting technique knit back and forth on the first 8 stitches in stocking stitch for 8 rows, beginning on a knit row and ending with a purl row. Knit back across these 8 stitches and add extra 3 stitches from the stitches on the left-hand needle (11 stitches in all). Purl back over 8 stitches only *. Repeat from * to * until all 26 stitches have been knitted in this manner. Knit 3 rows garter stitch and cast off.

◀ Wavy ripples

Wavy ripples. Cast on 11 stitches. Knit 2 rows garter stitch. * Knit 4 rows stocking stitch starting on a knit row. Knitting as for short row knitting technique knit back and forth on the first 7 stitches in stocking stitch for 12 rows, ending on a purl row. Knit 1 row on all 11 stitches *. Repeat from * to * but for this and every other alternate repeat commence the stocking stitch section with a purl row.

Ripple 2

The softly graduating natural colours of this beautiful yarn lend themselves perfectly to the subtle texturing of this autumnal scarf.

Knitting Note

The 2 edge stitches at left and right are always knit stitches, except the first stitch of every row, which is a slipstitch.

1 Cast on 20 sts with size 5mm (US 8) needles and knit 2 rows g st.

2 K12 rows st st.

3 K4 edge sts, K12 more st and turn the knitting.

4 P12 sts and turn.

5 K12 rows st st. Before turning the work on the 12th row pick up 12 loops from the first of these 12 rows onto the spare needle. The point of the needle should be facing in the same direction as the main needle. Turn the work: **a** **b**

6 K1 st from the spare needle and then the equivalent st from the main needle in one operation. K12 sts in total in this manner and then knit the 4 edge sts: **a** **b**.

7 K4 edge sts, P12 sts, K2 edge sts.

8 Repeat steps **2** to **7**, 30 times in all.

9 K11 rows st st.

10 K2 rows g st.

11 Cast off all sts. Neaten ends.

Materials
● 3 x 1³⁄₄oz (50g) balls of Noro Yarn **Silk Garden** shade 213

Equipment
● One pair 5mm (US 8) needles and 1 spare needle smaller in diameter than the main needles

Techniques
● Cast on and off
● Knit
● Purl
● Short row knitting
● Knitted in pintucks

5a

5b

6a

6b

Ripple 2 variations

▶ **Wedge-shape pintucks**

Short row knitting technique as described in
Workshop 2, Allsorts (page 42) is used to create
wedge shape sections first on the right and then
on the left of the knitting, each section being
divided by a pintuck. Cast on 18 stitches and knit
2 rows garter stitch. To make the first stocking
stitch wedge section, commence with a knit
row and knit back and forth across all 18stitches,
then 15 stitches, 12 stitches, 9 stitches, 6 stitches
and 3 stitches. Knit 2 rows garter stitch.
Commence pintuck with a knit row and knit 9
rows of stocking stitch in total ending with a knit
row. Knit a joining row and then 1 more row
across all 18 stitches. To make the next wedge
section repeat the sequence but this time
commencing wedge shape, pintuck and joining
row with a purl row. Repeat as required.

◀ **Ridges & furrows**

Garter stitch bands combine with stocking stitch
pintucks knitted in Noro Silk Garden shade 87
on 5mm (US 8) needles. Cast on 20 stitches and
knit 14 rows garter stitch. To knit the pintucks
commence with a purl row and continue to knit
in stocking stitch for 9 rows in total. Knit a joining
row across all 20 stitches. Repeat this sequence
as required.

▶ Knit facing pintucks

Partially linked knit facing pintucks. Cast on 15 stitches. Knit 2 rows garter stitch, 6 rows stocking stitch, 2 rows garter stitch and 12 rows stocking stitch. Make a joining row over the centre 5 stitches only. Repeat as required. Alternatively, try using this variation as purl facing.

◀ Off-set pintucks

Short row pintucks are knitted first to the right-hand side and then to the left. Cast on 15 stitches and knit 2 rows garter stitch. Knit 4 rows stocking stitch on all 15 stitches commencing with a knit row and 10 rows on 10 stitches only. Link these 10 stitches to form a pintuck and knit to the end of the row. Knit 4 rows stocking stitch commencing with a purl row and 10 rows on stitches only. Link these 10 stitches to form a pintuck and purl to the end of the row. Repeat as required.

WORKSHOP FIVE

Ice Queen

Knitted in modern lightweight yarns and decorated with big sequins and beads, these glitzy boas are a contemporary interpretation of the working method used to produce grand eyelets in traditional laces.

The simplest grand eyelets comprise a certain number of made stitches that are essentially multiple throws of the yarn over and around the needles, followed by a single multiple decrease. This sequence is then repeated at intervals across the row according to the pattern.

On the following row, the yarn overs are knitted into with first a knit stitch, and then a purl stitch, for as many times as is required to form the requisite number of new stitches. These new stitches compensate for the decreased stitches from the first row. For example if you purl 7 stitches together than you will need to make 6 new stitches using the yarn over method. The last remaining stitch on the needle after the multiple decrease brings the total number of stitches in this pattern unit back up to the original 7 stitches.

The secret of making a successful multiple decrease is to use a larger needle on the

row preceding the multiple decrease rows, reverting back to the original size needles for the latter. You will be able to transfer the large groups of stitches more easily if you work from a larger needle to a smaller needle.

You will also notice that the larger needle multiple decreases are written as purl decreases. It is much easier to insert the needle purl-wise to knit off a large number of stitches than knit-wise.
Try this simple example to clarify the technique. Cast on 19 stitches and knit three rows. Knit the third row loosely or on a larger needle than the previous rows to accommodate for the multiple decreases on the next row. Step 1: To knit the eyelet row work as follows: K2, bring the yarn forward as if to purl, * M4, P5tog *, repeat from * to * three times in all, K2. Step 2: The back row is knitted thus: K2 * K1 (K1, P1, K1 and P1 into the yarn overs) * and repeat from * to * three times in all, K2.

Ice Queen 1

Knitted sideways on circular needles to accommodate the large number of stitches cast on, this boa is easy to knit once you have mastered the art of making multiple decreases.

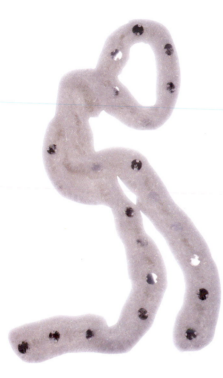

The boa measures approximately 86½in (220cm) long and 2¾in (7cm) wide.

Materials
- 2 x 1¾oz (50g) balls Stylecraft **Icicle Double Knitting**, shade white
- 30 round ¾in (20mm) silver sequins with side holes
- 60 small silver beads

Equipment
- 8mm (US 11) circular needles
- 10mm (US 15) circular needles
- Needle for sewing on sequins and beads

Techniques
- Cast on and off
- Knit
- Purl
- Multiple increases yarn over method
- Multiple decreases purl-wise
- Working with different size circular needles

Knitting Note
To make the boa shorter, deduct stitches in multiples of 7. One unit of pattern is 7 stitches wide and measures approximately 3in (7.5cm) in length and 2¾in (7cm) wide. The example given here comprises 28 units of 7 sts plus 2 extra sts at right and left edges.

Large silver sequins add sparkle to this glamourous boa.

3a

3b

3c

1 Using 8mm (US 11) circular needles cast on 200 sts with two ends of yarn and K2 rows.

2 Change to size 10mm (US 15) needles and K1 row. Change back to 8mm needles.

3 K2, * m6, P7tog *, repeat from * to * until 2 sts remain, K2: **a b c**.

4 K2, * K1, (K1, P1, K1, P1, K1, P1 into the made sts) *, repeat from * to * until 2 sts remain, K2.

5 K3 rows and cast off.

6 Attach the sequins and beads on either side of the grand eyelet. To do this you should first stitch up through the hole in the sequin from the back of the knitting, then through the hole in the bead, and finally back down through the sequin into the back of the knitting. Neaten the ends of the sewing thread.

Ice Queen 1 variations

▶ Mirror images in white & silver

A is Stylecraft white **Icicle** yarn and **B** is Wendy **Velvet Touch** Shade 1400 White Velvet.

1 Using 6mm (US 10) needles cast on 24 sts and K2 rows **B** and 1 row **A**.

2 Continue knitting with **B**, K1, * m1, K2tog *, repeat from * to * until 1 st remains, K1.

3 K2 rows **A**, 4 rows **B** and 1 row A

4 Change to 9mm needles and K1 row **A**

5 Change back to 7mm needles. K4, * m3, P4tog*, repeat from * to * 4 times in all, K4

6 K4, * K1 (P1, K1, P1 into made stitch)*, repeat from * to * 4 times in all, K4.

7 The remainder of the sample is a mirror image of the first section.

◀ Silver & white sparkles

A is Texere **Stardust** in Silver and **B** is 2 strands of Stylecraft white **Icicle**.

1 Using 6mm (US 10) needles cast on 26 sts with yarn **A**.

2 Continue knitting with **A**, K1, * m1, K2tog *, repeat from * to * until 1 st remains, K1. K1 row.

3 K4 rows **B** and 1 row **A**.

4 Change to 9mm (US 13) needles and knit 24 sts and K2 together. 25 sts remain on the needles.

5 Change back to 6mm needles. K5, * m4, P5tog*, repeat from * to * 3 times in all, K5.

6 K5, * K1 (P1, K1, P1, K1 into made st)*, repeat from * to * 3 times in all, K5.

7 K2 rows **A** and 4 rows **B**.

8 K24 sts, knit into the front and the back of the next st. 26 sts remain on the needle.

9 Repeat step 2 and cast off.

▶ White on white decorated with silver beads & sequins

Knitted in three different textures of white and silver yarn this sample is knitted in the same manner as sample 1 and decorated with small silver sequins and facetted silver beads.

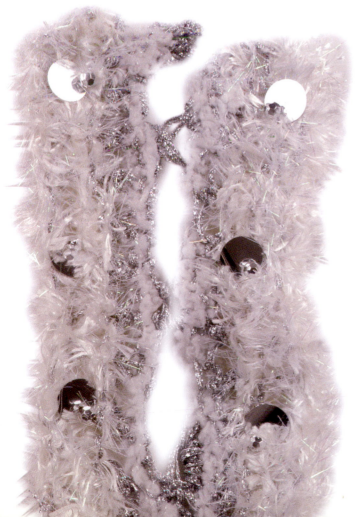

◀ Grand eyelets combined with small eyelets

Knitted in four strongly contrasting textures of white and silver yarns this sample combines grand eyelets with rows of single eyelets knitted in silver.

Ice Queen 2

Many variations to this boa are possible; for example, by changing the number of stitches and rows between each eyelet or the number of stitches increased and decreased at any one time. The same pattern sequence can look very different knitted up in a variety of different weights and textures of yarn (see the examples on pages 86–87 developed from the main boa patterns).

This boa is approximately 86½in (220cm) long and 5in (12.5cm) wide.

Materials
- 1 x 1¾oz (50g) ball each of **A** – **Amelie** shade 03, **B** – **Icicle** by Stylecraft in pale pink and **C** – **Snowdrift** by Stylecraft in pale pink.
- 30 White Pearl ¾in (20mm) round sequins
- 60 small iridescent white beads

Equipment
- 1 pair each of 7mm (US 10.5/11) and 9mm (US 13) needles

Techniques
- Cast on and off
- Knit
- Purl
- Multiple increases yarn over method
- Multiple decreases purl-wise
- Working with different needle sizes
- Changing colours at regular intervals

Knitting Notes

Leave the yarn that is not in use attached to the knitting, also taking care not to pull the new yarns tight when one colour is exchanged for the other.

A is knitted as a single end throughout, **B** and **C** are knitted together throughout and are exchanged one for the other every two rows.

Pearlised sequins softly catch the light to add movement and texture to the boa.

1 Using 7mm (US 10.5/11) needles cast on 16 sts with colours **B** plus **C** and K2 rows.

2 Change to 9mm (US 13) needles and knit one row. Leave **B** and **C** attached to the knitting.

3 Change to 7mm (US 10.5/11) needles and **A** work as follows: K2, bring yarn forward as if to purl, * m5 **a**, P6tog * **b c d e**, repeat from * to * twice in all, K2.

4 K2, * K1, (K1, P1, K1, P1, K1 into the made stitch dropping a loop each time you make a new stitch **a b c d**) *, repeat from * to * twice in all, K2. Leave **A** attached to the knitting.

5 Change to 9mm (US 13) needles and **B** plus **C** and knit one row.

6 Repeat steps **3** to **5** but at the same time exchanging colours every 2 rows.

7 Repeat until the ball of **A** is finished.

8 Cast off.

9 Decorate with sequins.

3d

4b

3e

4c

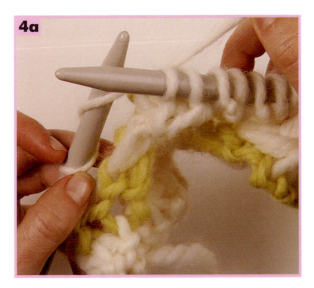

4a

4d

Ice Queen 2 variations

▶ Eyelet with extra knit stitch

In this sample additional rows are knitted between each repeat of the eyelet pattern and an extra knit stitch is worked before each group of made stitches when compared to the main boa pattern resulting in a bulkier fabric.

1 Using 5mm (US 8) needles cast on 24sts .

2 Change to 6mm (US 10) needles and K one row.

3 Change to 5mm needles. Work as follows: K2, * K1, bring yarn forward as if to purl, m3, K4 tog *, repeat from * to * until 2 sts remain, K2.

4 K2, * K1, (K1, P1, K1, into the made stitch) K1*, repeat from * to * until 2 sts remain, K2.

5 Knit 2 rows.

6 Change to 6mm needles and knit one row.

7 Repeat steps **2** to **6** as required.

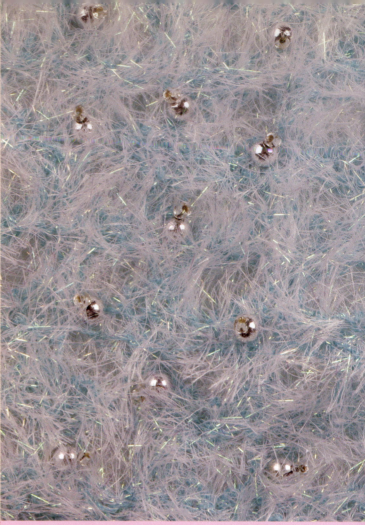

◀ Lightweight openwork pattern

A more openwork fabric than Sample 1 and lighter in weight than the main boa design this example is knitted in a single end of Stylecraft **Icicle** in pink.

1 Using 6mm (US 10) needles cast on 20sts

2 Change to 7mm (US 10.5/11) needles and knit one row.

3 Change back to 6mm needles and work as follows: K2, bring yarn forward as if to purl, * m3, K4tog *, repeat from * to * until 2 sts remain, K2.

4 K2, * K1, (K1, P1, K1, into the made stitch) *, repeat from * to * until 2 sts remain, K2.

5 Change to 7mm and knit one row.

6 Repeat steps **2** to **5** as required.

▶ Simple eyelets in two colours

A simple interpretation of the grand eyelet principle knitted in two colours, which are exchanged every two rows. The stitch pattern is worked in multiples of 5 sts plus 4 edge sts by 3 rows.

First pattern row K2, bring yarn forward as if to purl, * m4, P5tog *, repeat from * to * until 2 sts remain, K2.

Second pattern row K2, * K1, (K1, P1, K1, P1 into the made stitch) *, repeat from * to * until 2 sts remain, K2.

Third pattern row K1 row only on a larger size needle.

◀ Large eyelets with sequins

Knitted in Wendy **Velvet Touch** and **Snowdrift** combined with **Icicle** (both from Stylecraft) the eyelets in this design are shifted 2 stitches to the left or the right on every other repeat.

1 Using 7mm (US 10.5/11) needles cast on 22sts.
2 Change to 9mm (US 13) needles. Knit one row.
3 Change to 7mm needles and work as follows: K1, bring yarn forward as if to purl, * m5, P6tog *, repeat from * to * until 3 sts remain, K3.
4 K3, * K1, (K1, P1, K1, K1, P1into the made stitch) K1*, repeat from * to * until 1 st remains, K1.
5 Change to 9mm and K1 row.
6 Change back to 7mm needles and work as follows: K3, bring yarn forward as if to purl, * m5, P6tog *, repeat from * to * until 1 st remain, K1.
7 K1, * K1, (K1, P1, K1, K1, P1 into the made stitch) K1*, repeat from * to * until 3 sts remain, K3.
8 Change to 9mm and K1 row.
9 Repeat steps **3** to **8** as required.

Lattice

Openwork meshes knitted in slinky viscose and glittery yarns combine the drape and handle of contemporary fibres with a thoroughly modern interpretation of traditional lace knitting techniques.

New techniques introduced in this workshop show you how to create openwork stitch patterns using the principles of increasing and decreasing decoratively. The small eyelets are formed at regular intervals in the knitting by increasing and then making a decrease to compensate for this new stitch.

The way the increase is made depends on whether the made stitch is situated between a knit and a purl stitch, or between two knit stitches or two purl stitches.

On a knit row bringing the yarn forward as if to purl makes the new stitch before the next stitch is worked knit-wise or a knit decrease. This manoeuvre is abbreviated to M1. To do the same thing after a knit stitch but before a purl stitch or a purl decrease bring the yarn forward then take it over and around the needle and back to the front of the work again. Insert the needle purl-wise into the next stitch and purl it (or P2tog).

A decrease can be made either before or after the made stitch in one of two ways. Either by working two stitches together (K2tog or P2tog) or knitting as follows: slip 1 stitch, knit 1 stitch and pass the slipstitch over. The latter is abbreviated to SL1, K1, PSSO. The purl version of this is SL 1, P1, PSSO.

Notice how the openwork sections of the boa in Lattice 1 appear to move first to the left and then to the right. This built-in slant or bias depends on the placement of the made stitch in relationship to the decreased stitches. If the made stitch is before the decrease (M1, K2tog) then the bias is to the right. If the reverse is true (K2tog, M1) then the bias is to the left when the work is facing the knitter.

Lattice 1

The first project of this workshop exploits a built-in bias found in certain types of openwork patterns to create a zigzag-shaped edge.

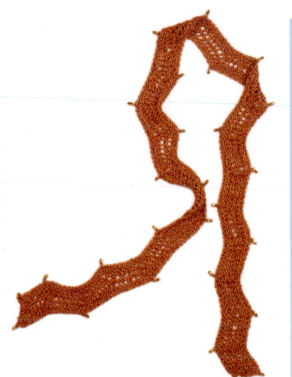

Materials
- 1 x 3 ½oz (100g) cone **A** – Texere **Stardust** shade Tango
- 1 x 3 ½oz (100g) cone **B** – Texere **Prism** shade Tango
- ½in (12mm) drop beads in gold
- Small round gold beads

Equipment
- 1 pair 4mm (US 6) knitting needles.

Techniques
- Cast on and off
- Knit
- Purl
- Made stitches (yarn over)
- Decreasing knit 2 together
- Decreasing PSSO (pass the slip stitch over)

Knitting Note

This project exploits the left and right bias in a moderately easy-to-knit eyelet pattern. The first section of the pattern has a bias to the right. The made stitch (yarn over method) precedes the decrease. This sequence is repeated all the way across the row. The back row is purled excepting the two edge stitches at left and right that are always knit stitches. These two rows are then repeated for a given number of rows. The second section of the pattern is left biased. Here the decreases are knitted before each of the made stitches and the back row purled and knitted as before.

Small drop beads bring out the gold tones of the yarn and add texture and weight.

1 Cast on 11 sts in yarns **A** plus **B** and knit 1 row.

2 K2, K1, * m1 , K2tog * , repeat from * to * 3 times in all, K2.

3 K2, P7, K2.

4 Repeat steps **2** and **3** eight times in all.

5 K2, *SL1 , K1 , psso , m1 * , repeat from * to * three times in all, K1, K2.

6 K2, P7, K2.

7 Repeat steps **5** and **6**, **8** times in all.

8 Repeat steps **2** to **7**, 12 times in all and cast off.

Lattice 1 variations

▶ Zigzag mesh

Zigzag mesh in Texere **Prism** (Shade Mint) and Texere **Stardust**. The openwork design is repeated five times across the row to make a broader strip of knitting. Each bias section is made proportionately longer to balance out the new width.

1 Using 4mm (US 6) needles cast on 15 sts with one strand each of Texere **Prism** and Texere **Stardust** and K1 row.

2 K2, K1, * m1, K2tog *, repeat from * to * 5 times in all, K2.

3 K2, P11, K2.

4 Repeat steps **2** and **3**, 12 times in all.

5 K2, *SL1, K1, PSSO, m1 *, repeat from * to * five times in all, K1, K2.

6 K2, P11, K2.

7 Repeat steps **5** and **6**, 8 times in all.

8 Repeat steps **2** to **7** as many times as is required and cast off.

◀ Zigzag openwork pattern in all rows knit

Zigzag openwork pattern in all rows knit. Knitted in a mix of Texere **Prism** (shade Mint) and Rowan **Lurex Shimmer** in pale blue over 15 sts, this variation is similar to sample 1 except that the odd rows are knit rather than purl rows and each section of the pattern is repeated 9 times only.

▶ Narrow zigzag border

A narrow zigzag border knitted over 11 stitches.
The openwork stitch pattern is repeated first to
the right and then to the left with each section
being 6 repeats in all divided by a single row of
eyelets bordered by knit rows. To work this
section first K2 rows then make a row of eyelets
thus: K2, K1, * m1, K2tog *, repeat from * to *
until 2 sts remain, K2. K1 row.

◀ Openwork zigzags with centre panel of stocking stitch

Openwork zigzags with centre panel in stocking
stitch. The openwork pattern is divided by a
central band of stocking stitch that is always
knitted over the same three stitches. The two
stitches at the left and right edges are knit
stitches throughout.

1 Cast on 17sts.
2 K2. K1, m1, K2tog, m1, K2tog. K3. K1, m1,
   K2tog, m1, K2tog. K2.
3 K2, P13, K2.
4 Repeat steps 1 and 2, 15 times in all.
5 K2. * S11, K1, psso, m1 *, repeat from * to *
   twice in all, K1. K3. * S11, K1, psso, m1 *,
   repeat from * to * twice in all, K1. K2.
6 K2, P13, K2.
7 Repeat steps **2** to **6** as many times as required
   and cast off.

Lattice 2

This project workshop combines a narrow border pattern of small-scale eyelets and lace points with grand eyelets. The latter are knitted in the same way as the grand eyelets described in Workshop 5, Ice Queen (pages 81–93).

Materials
- 1 cone each of **A** – Texere **Stardust** shade Kingfisher and **B** – Texere **Prism** shade Peacock

Equipment
- 1 pair 4mm (US 6) needles

Techniques
- Cast on and off
- Knit
- Purl
- Made stitches worked thus: Bring the yarn forward then take it over and around the needle and back to the front of the work again
- P2tog (purl 2 together)

Knitting Notes

Odd-numbered rows in the pattern are broken down into separate units relating first to the border stitches and then to the triangular point with grand eyelet.

The straight-section border pattern is knitted on the same number of stitches throughout. The zigzag points are increased by one stitch on every other row, always at the same position in the knitting, and then the same numbers of stitches are cast off in one operation to reduce the number of stitches back to the number originally cast on. At the same time, the grand eyelets are introduced into the pointed section as it is being increased in size. This is the step where the pattern asks you to make a large number of made stitches on one row and in the subsequent row knit and purl several times into this long made stitch to create the grand eyelet.

Octopus

Workshop Seven is all about exploiting the new generation of lightweight feathery eyelash yarns, knitted on their own or in combination one with the other, into glamorous boas for that special night out.

Dramatic and frond-like, these boas are designed to let the yarns speak for themselves. The easy-to-knit patterns utilize just three techniques: casting on, casting off and simple knit stitches. More complex stitch patterns would simply be lost in these lush, dense textures.

The shaped fronds are knitted using a simple method of casting stitches on and then off around a central core of stitches that are retained throughout. In both the main projects, the fronds are knitted by casting on extra stitches, then knitting a couple of rows over this increased number of stitches before casting back off these extra stitches.

You can of course alter the long length of the fronds by casting on and off more or fewer stitches, or by making the central core wider or narrower by adding or subtracting to the number of stitches as written in the pattern. Vary the depth of the fronds or the central core by knitting more or fewer rows than given.

Octopus 1

The first project in this workshop features quick-to-knit yarns worked on big needles and with the frond length the same over the full length of the boa.

Materials
- 4 x 1¾oz (50g) balls in Elle **Plume** in shade 222. Used 2 strand throughout.

Equipment
- 1 pair 10mm (US 15) needles

Techniques
- Cast on and off using around thumb method
- Knit

1 Using 10mm (US 15) needles cast on 27 sts.

2 K3 rows.

3 Cast off 10 sts at the beginning of next row and continue to knit to end of row: **a** **b**. (17 sts remain.)

3a

3b

Knitting Note
Colour **A** is used 2 strand throughout.

4 Cast off 10 more sts at
beginning of next row and
continue to knit to end of row:
a **b**. (7 sts remain.)

5

6a

6b

5 K5 rows on these 7 sts.

6 K1 row and cast back on 10
sts using thumb method of
casting on at the end of this
row: **a** **b**. (17 sts remain.)

7 Knit these 17 sts and cast
back on a further 10 sts at
end of row: **a** **b**. (27 sts
remain.)

8 Repeat steps **2** to **6**, until the
yarn runs out ending on step **2**.

9 Cast off all sts and stitch in
any loose ends.

7a

7b

Octopus 1 variations

▶ Velvety multicoloured fronds

All variations are knitted in a similar manner to the main boa pattern showing how the design would look in alternative yarns, and with only slight variations made to the numbers of stitches and rows worked. Different needle sizes are chosen depending upon the thickness of the yarn mixes. Knitted to exactly the same pattern as the main boa, but on 12mm (US 17) needles and in a beautifully soft multicoloured yarn called **Intention**, shade 02 from GGH.

◀ Quick-to-knit luxurious fronds

A thicker, more densely textured variation of the boa pattern, this time knitted in 2 strands of Patons **Whisper**, shade 00013 plied with 1 strand of **Intention** shade 02. The fronds are 2 rows deep whilst the centre core is knitted over 5 rows.

▶ Soft & lush fronds

Knitted on 12mm (US17) needles this example is a thinner variation of Sample 2, knitted in 1 strand of Patons **Whisper**, shade 00014 plied with 1 strand of **Intention**. The fronds are 3 rows deep whilst the centre core is knitted over 5 rows.

◀ Densely textured fronds

Knitted in **Milan** from Stylecraft, this soft, densely textured sample was knitted on 10mm (US 15) needles. The fronds are 2 rows deep and the central core 5 rows.

Octopus 2

This second project is knitted in thinner yarns and on finer needles. The lengths of the fronds are varied, graduating from short to long and then back again to short.

Materials
- 2 x 1¾oz (50g) balls **A** – Sirdar **Fizz** shade Fiesta
- 1 x 1¾oz (50g) balls each of Stylecraft **Eskimo** in shades **B** – 5480 Kingfisher, **C** – 5482 Fusion and **D** – 5483 Jade.

Equipment
- 1 pair size 7mm (US10.5/11) needles

Techniques
- Cast on and off using around thumb method
- Knit
- Knitting with 2 colours

Knitting Notes
Figures in brackets refer to the different lengths of fronds. The boa comprises 3 fronds of 5 stitches, 5 fronds of 8 stitches, 8 fronds of 13 stitches, 13 fronds of 21 stitches, 8 fronds of 13 stitches, 5 fronds of 8 stitches and 3 fronds of 5 stitches. There is an additional core of 3 stitches that are knitted throughout.

Colour **A** is knitted throughout and combined with either colour **B**, **C** or **D**. Exchange these colours after every third frond.

1 Using 7mm (US 10.5/11) needles cast on 8 sts.

2 Cast off 5 sts at beg of next row and continue to knit to end of the row, 3 sts remain on the needle.

3 K2 rows.

4 K1 more row. Cast on 5 sts at the end of the row using the thumb method of casting on.

5 Repeat steps **2** to **4** once more and steps **2** to **3** once more. 3 sts remain on the needle.

6 K1 row on these 3 sts. Cast on 8 (13: 21: 13: 8: 5) sts at the end of the row using the thumb method of casting on.

7 Cast off (13: 21: 13: 8: 5) sts beginning of next row and continue to knit to end of row, 3 sts remain on the needles.

8 K2 rows.

9 K1 more row on these 3 sts. Cast on 8 (13: 21: 13: 8: 5) sts at the end of the row using the thumb method of casting on.

10 Repeat steps **7** to **9**, 4 (7: 12: 7: 4: 3) times in all and steps **7** to **8** once more except on the final frond which ends at step **7**. Cast off the remaining 3 sts instead of knitting them.

Octopus 2 variations

▶ Fluffy fronds of varied lengths

This is knitted in one shade of Colinette **Firecracker** yarn on 12mm (US 17) needles. Follow the pattern in terms of rows and stitches.

◀ Multicoloured fronds

This repeats the pattern of the first variation, but uses a mix of bright funky colours of Colinette **Firecracker** yarn on 12mm (US 17) needles. Follow the pattern in terms of rows and stitches.

▶ Hot pink fronds

Colinette **Firecracker** with **Amalfi** multicoloured tape yarn on 12mm (US 17) needles. Follow the pattern in terms of rows and stitches.

◀ Fronds in alternating colours

Colinette **Firecracker** with **Amalfi** multicoloured tape yarn on 12mm (US 17) needles. Follow the pattern in terms of rows and stitches.

Reef

The frond-like extensions are knitted by casting on and off the same number of stitches at various points across a row. They can be made longer or shorter by casting on and off more or fewer stitches, packed closely together or spaced more widely. You can also make the fronds wider by knitting 2 or more rows on the new stitches before knitting the cast off row.

In *Reef 1*, the pattern asks you to cast on and off 8 stitches every alternate stitch thus: * Knit 2 stitches, slip the last stitch knitted back onto the left-hand needle. Cast on 8 stitches then cast them off again. *

This is how you do it: Do not count the stitch you have just transferred to the left needle as a new stitch. To make the first new stitch, insert the right-hand needle into this loop and pass the yarn around the needle as if to knit. Knit the stitch, drawing through the new loop and slipping it onto the left needle to form a new stitch. Repeat this operation until you have 8 new stitches on the left needle.

To cast off knit the first 2 stitches of this group of 8 stitches. Draw the loop of the first stitch over the second stitch, leaving 1 stitch from this group of 8 stitches on the right-hand needle. Knit the next stitch, then draw the first stitch over the needle. One stitch of this group will remain on the right-hand needle.

Continue to work thus until all of the 8 new stitches have been cast back off. The stitch you slipped from right-hand to left-hand needle at the beginning of this sequence should now be on the right needle.

Reef 1

The extra stitches are cast on and off using two needles in much the same way as you would make a two-needle cast on and off at the beginning and end of a piece of knitting.

Materials
- 4 x 1¾oz (50g) balls of **A** – Wendy **Shimmer** in shade Lagoon (2046)
- 1 x 1¾oz (50g) ball of **B** – Wendy **Velvet Touch** in shade Rich Turquoise (2054)

Equipment
- 1 pair 8mm (US 11) needles and 1 spare 8mm (US 11) needle

Techniques
- Cast on and off using 2 needles
- Knit
- Purl

Knitting Notes

Note the boa is knitted in two pieces and joined at centre back.

Wind off a ball of **Velvet Touch** so that you can knit 2 ends together where indicated.

A is knitted 2 strand, **B** is knitted 2 strand, **C** is knitted 1 strand.

1 Using 8mm needles cast on 11 sts with **A**, leave yarn attached.

2 Change to **C** and knit frond row thus: * K2 sts **a**, slip the last stitch knitted back onto the left-hand needle. Cast on 8 sts then cast them off again. * You should be left with 2 sts on the right-hand needle and 9 sts on the left–hand needle. Repeat from * to * until just one stitch remains. K1. Check that you still have 11 sts on the needle **b** **c** **d** **e**.

3 Knit 3 rows **B** and 8 rows **A**.

4 Repeat steps **2** to **3** three times in all.

5 Change to **C** and knit frond row thus: * K2 sts, slip the last stitch knitted back onto the left-hand needle. Cast on 5 sts then cast them off again. * You should be left with 2 sts on the right-hand needle and 9 sts on the left-hand needle. Repeat from * to * until just one stitch remains. K1. Check that you still have 11 sts on the needle.

6 As step **3**.

7 Repeat steps **5** to **6**, 5 times in all.

8 K24 rows **A**. Leave sts on the needle.

9 Knit a second half in the same manner until step **8**. K25 rows and leave sts on needle.

10 To knit the separate pieces together hold the work so that right sides are facing and both needles are parallel to each other and pointing in the same direction. Using a separate needle knit a stitch from the front needle with a stitch from the back needle. 11 sts remain. **a** **b**

11 Cast off these 11 sts.

12 Neaten all loose ends.

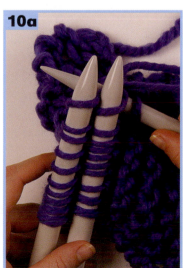

Reef 1 variations

▶ Frond border pattern

This sample shows how the frond design might be used as a border pattern repeated at either end of a long boa. Knit the main section in simple four rows stripe pattern described below.

Using 7mm (US 10.5/11) needles cast on 20 sts in **A** and knit one row. Knit a row of fronds on every alternate stitch casting on and off 8 extra stitches as described above. K7 rows in 2 strands of **B** and 2 rows in **A**. Repeat frond row. K10 rows in 2 strands of B and 2 rows in **A**. Repeat frond row.

Stripe pattern: * K2 rows **A** and 2 rows **B** (2 strand) *. Repeat from * to * as required.

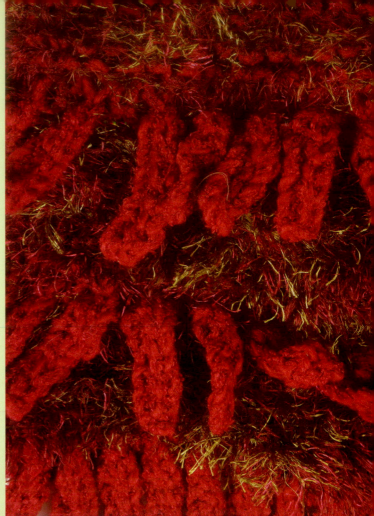

◀ Fluffy fronds with eyelash textures

Fluffy fronds combine with lush eyelash textures for a quick-knit boa. To knit a similar piece you will need 1 x 1¾oz (50g) ball each of **A** and **C** and 2 balls of **B** to make a short boa from this sample length.

Using 10mm (US 15) needles cast on 15 sts one strand each of **A** and **C**. K1 row. * Continue working in these two yarns, knit a row of fronds on every third stitch casting on and off 13 extra stitches as described above. Change to two strand of **B** combined with one strand of **C** and knit 13 rows, followed by 2 rows of **A** *.

Repeat from * to * making the fronds progressively shorter (8, 5 and then 3 stitches).

To make the second half of this short boa knit a mirror image reversing the instructions as given ending with a frond row of 13 stitches cast on and off.

▶ Quick-knit fluffy fronds

Fronds combine with elongated knit stitches (see Workshop 1, *Relax 2*, page 36) for another quick-knit fluffy boa.

Using 20mm (US 35/36) needles and one strand each of **A** and **B** cast on 20 sts and K1 row. Make a frond row (8 stitches on alternate stitches). * K1 row elongated knit and 1 row normal knit stitch *. Repeat from * to * three times in all. Knit one more elongated row. Make a frond row (8 stitches on alternate stitches).

Change to one strand of **B** knitted with 2 strands of **C** for 2 rows. Make a frond row (8 stitches on alternate stitches). K2 rows. * K1 row elongated knit and 1 row normal knit stitch *. Repeat from * to * as required.

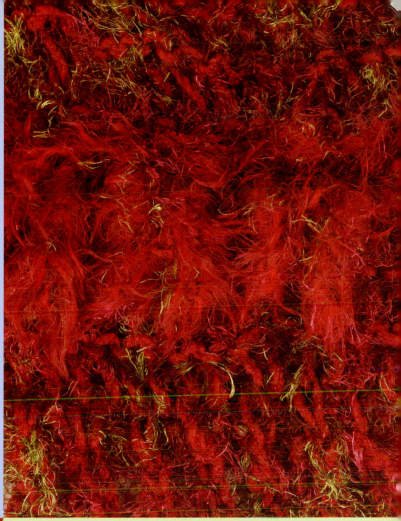

◀ Short fronds with openwork stitch pattern

An openwork base fabric in elongated stitches decorated with short fronds (5 sts are cast on and off every second stitch) and knitted in a mix of **A**, **B** and **C**.

Reef 2

Knitted sideways on, this colourful boa is worked in bright hues and contrasting modern textures with a hint of sparkle for party wear. The frond rows are knitted in the same manner as for Reef 1. New for this project is the introduction of slipped stitches as part of the pattern.

Materials

- 1 x 1¾oz (50g) ball **A** – **Stars** from GGH in shade 05
- 1 x 3½oz (100g) hank of **B** – **Firecracker** from Colinette Yarns in Magenta
- 4 x 11yd (10m) skeins of **C** – Texere **Vision** ribbon in red

Equipment

- 1 circular knitting needle 7.5mm (US 10.5/11)

Techniques

- Cast on and off using 2 needles
- Knit
- Purl
- Slip stitch purl-wise

Knitting Note
C is used 2 strand throughout.

1 Using 7.5cm (US 10.5/11) circular knitting needles cast on 144 sts in **A** and K1 row.

2 Knit a row of fronds on every fourth stitch casting on and off 8 extra stitches as described above for *Reef 1*, in **A**.

3 K1 row **A** and 2 rows **C**.

4 Change to colour **B**, * K1, slip 1*. Repeat from * to * until all sts have been worked in this manner. Do this for 2 rows. On the second row you should be knitting the slipped stitches

from the previous row and slipping the knit stitches.

5 K2 rows **A**.

6 As step **2**.

7 K2 rows each of **A** and **C**.

8 As step **4**.

9 K1 row **A**.

10 As step **2**.

11 Cast off. Neaten ends.

Reef 2 variations

▶ All the blues

All the variations follow similar pattern sequences to the main boa. The changes are made through choosing to work with yarns textures exploiting the new ribbon yarns to the full and mixing like-coloured yarns from different sources to customize the colour range. All the swatches were knitted on 8mm (US 11) needles over 30 stitches. Knitted in mid-tone blues of a similar colour bias this sample explores the contrast between the textures of the feathery eyelash yarn and the changing surfaces of the metallic colours. Here one strand of Texere **Stardust** (shade Kingfisher) is plied with GGH **Stars** for the fronds and then knitted as a contrast to Elle **Plume** in shade 217 used 2 strand in the slip stitch sections.

◀ Ribbon & glitz combined

A colour harmony of mid-tone blues and greens where the lush texture and colour of Colinette **Firecracker** yarn (shade Jay) is picked up in the mix of glitzy colours. The latter comprises two ends of Twilley's **Goldfingering** shade 5 and one end of GGH **Stars** in blue.

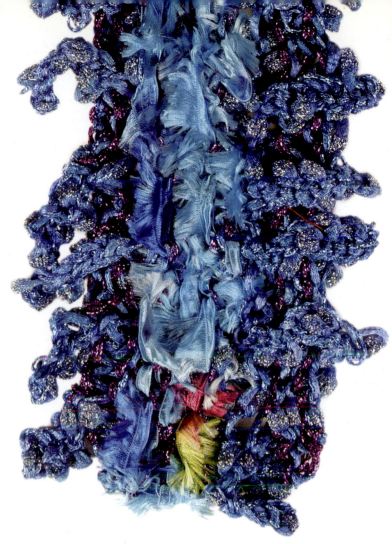

▶ Contrasting textures in blues & purples

A blue and purple colour mix giving combing three different textures. The fronds are knitted in one strand each of mid-tone blue Texere **Stardust** (shade Kingfisher) and GGH **Stars**. The slip stitch section is knitted in a combination of purple metallic colours (three ends combined together of Twilley's **Goldfingering** and Rowan **Shimmer** yarn) contrasting with Colinette **Firecracker** yarn.

◀ Multicoloured variation

A wider range of colours is added to this final sample through the introduction of **Amalfi** multi-coloured tape yarn contrasting with Colinette **Firecracker** and the blue metallic yarns from Sample 1.

131

Lagoon

Think of this collection of scarves as giant braids – a contemporary interpretation of the finely worked insertions which would have traditionally been knitted in fine cotton. They might originally have been used for edging household linen, but here, knitted in modern ribbon and tape yarns, they are decorated with metal and paua shell beads.

The garter-stitch triangles in these patterns are knitted at an angle to the straight section, and are made by first increasing one stitch on every other row, for example 9 times (18 rows) and then casting off these 9 stitches in one operation.

The increases are made immediately after the straight section at the same point in the knitting on every other row. These new stitches follow on after the point where the work is increased, adding extra length to the knitting, which in turn becomes the edge of the garter stitch triangle.

Lagoon 1

The patterns, while not for the absolute beginner, are not complicated to knit just so long as you break the design down into small units. A word of warning though: a little concentration is required until the pattern begins to take shape.

Materials
- 1 x 3½oz (100g) hank of **A** – Colinette **Giotto** shade 135 Sahara
- 1 x 3½oz (100g) hank of **B** – Colinette **Enigma** shade 135 Sahara
- 35 barrel-shaped metal beads approximately ½in (1cm) in length
- 6 long metal beads approximately 1½in (4cm) in length
- 70 small round metal beads bigger than the holes in the barrel-shaped beads.
- 12 round beads bigger than the holes in the long metal beads

Equipment
- 1 pair 6mm (US 10) needles

Techniques
- Casting on and off
- Knit
- Purl
- Made stitches (yarn over method)
- Knitting with alternating colours of yarn every 2 rows

Knitting Note
It is not necessary to break off the yarns at the end of rows when not in use, just twist one colour around the other before exchanging the colours every two rows.

1 Using 6mm (US 10) needles cast on 16 sts and K2 rows in yarn **A** and 2 rows **B**.

2 In **A**, K4, * M1, K2 tog * Repeat from * to * twice in all, K4, M1, K2 tog, M1, K2 (17 stitches).

3 In **A** K3, P2, K4, P4, K4. Leave **A** attached to the knitting.

4 **B** K4, * m1, K2 tog * Repeat from * to * twice in all, K4, m1, K2 tog, M1, K3 (18 sts).

5 In **B** K4, P2, K4, P4, K4. Leave **B** attached to the knitting.

6 Continue in this manner, increasing the number of sts by one on every even numbered row until there are 25 sts on the needle.

6 Next row is an odd-numbered row. Cast off 9 sts, K2 to include loop left on needle after cast off is completed, P2, K4, P4, K4.

8 Go back to step **2** and repeat as many times as required.

9 K2 rows **B** and 2 rows **A**. Cast off. Neaten loose ends.

2a

2b

2c

2d

Lagoon 1 variations

▶ **Garter stitch triangles with narrow edging in two colours**

1 Using 6mm (US 10) needles cast on 10 sts and K2 rows in **A**.

2 A * K2 m1, K2tog * repeat from * to * twice in all. m1, K2 (11 sts)

3 A K3, * P2, K2 * repeat from * to * twice

4 B * K2 m1, K2tog * repeat from * to * twice in all. m1, K3 (12 sts).

5 B K4, * P2, K2 * repeat from * to * twice

Continue in this manner, increasing the number of sts by one on every even-numbered row until there are 24 sts on the needle. Next row is an odd-numbered row. Cast off 14 stitches, K2 to include loop left on needle after cast off is completed, P2, K2, P2, K2. Go back to step **2** and repeat as many times as required.

◀ **Deep border in openwork pattern with garter stitch triangles**

1 Using 7mm (US 10.5/11) needles cast on 16 sts and K2 rows in **A**.

2 K6, * m1, K2 tog * repeat from * to * 4 times in all, m1, K2 (17 sts).

3 K3, P8, K6.

4 K6, * m1, K2 tog * repeat from * to * 4 times in all, m1, K3 (18 sts).

5 K4, P8, K6.

Continue in this manner, increasing the number of stitches by one on every even-numbered row until there are 24 sts on the needle. Next row is an odd-numbered row. Cast off 8 sts, K2 to include loop left on needle after cast off is completed, P8, K6. Go back to step **2** and repeat as many times as required.

▶ Narrow border pattern in ribbon and tape yarns

1 Using 6mm (US 10) needles cast on 10 sts and K2 rows in **A** and 2 rows in **B**.

2 A K4 * m1, K2tog * repeat from * to * twice in all, m1, K2 (11 stitches).

3 A K3, P4, K4.

4 B K4 * m1, K2tog * repeat from * to * twice in all, m1, K3 (12 stitches).

5 B K4, P4, K4.

Continue in this manner, increasing the number of sts by one on every even-numbered row until there are 19 sts on the needle. Next row is an odd-numbered row. Cast off 9 sts, K2 to include loop left on needle after cast off is completed, P4, K4. Go back to step **2** and repeat as many times as required.

◀ Wide border pattern in ribbon and tape yarn

1 Using 6mm (US 10) needles cast on 18 sts and knit 2 rows in **A** and 2 rows in **B**.

2 A *K4, m1, K2tog, m1, K2tog * repeat from * to * twice in all, m1, K2 (19 sts).

3 A K3, * P4, K4 * repeat from * to * twice in all.

4 B *K4, m1, K2tog, K4, m1, K2tog * repeat from * to * twice in all, m1, K3 (20 stitches).

5 B K4, * P4, K4 * repeat from * to * twice in all.

Continue in this manner, increasing the number of sts by one on every even-numbered row until there are 27 sts on the needle. Next row is an odd-numbered row. Cast off 9 sts, K2 to include loop left on needle after cast off is completed, P4, K4, P4, K4. Go back to step **2** and repeat as many times as required.

Lagoon 2

Worked short ways on the straight section of the braid, above the garter stitch triangles is a simple eyelet pattern not unlike the construction of the openwork patterns in Workshop 6, Lattice (page 94), and is knitted on the same number of stitches throughout. Here the increases and decreases are for decorative purposes only.

This scarf is approximately 71in (180cm) long by 1½in (4cm) wide at the narrowest point and 2¾in (7cm) wide at the deepest point.

Materials
- 1 x 3½oz (100g) hank **A** – Colinette **Enigma** shade 85 (Jay)
- 1 x 3½oz (100g) cone **B** – Texere **Stardust** in shade deep mauve
- ¾in (20mm) paua shell discs with holes

Equipment
- 1 pair 6mm (US 10) knitting needles
- Sewing needle to go through holes in shell decorations

Techniques
- Cast on and off
- Knit
- Purl
- Made stitches (yarn over method)

Knitting Notes

The unit of repeat for this pattern is approximately 6⅔in (17cm) wide.

There are 9 increases worked one at a time on every odd row number, 9 times in all for one side of the point. Once this stage is completed you will commence casting off these same 9 sts on the next even-numbered row until you are left with 9 sts. This is the same number of sts that were cast on at the start of the pattern.

Note that to keep the repeat of the openwork mesh pattern correct every other odd-numbered row ends with a K1 (rows 1, 5, and 9 for example) whilst rows 3, 7 and 11 for example end with a K2 together.

The beaded points of this zigzag scarf hang beautifully when it is worn around the waist.

1 Cast on 9 sts using 6mm (US 10) needles with **A** plus **B**. K2, m1, K2tog, K1. m1 (this is the place in the row where the increases and decreases take place to make the points). K1, * m1, K2tog *. Repeat from * to * until 1 st remains. K1 **a** **b**. There should be 10 stitches on the needle.

2 Knit back over 5 sts until 5 sts remain on the needle. P3, K2.

1a

1b

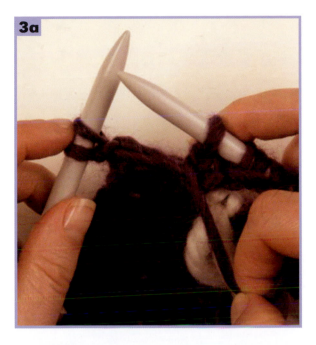

3a

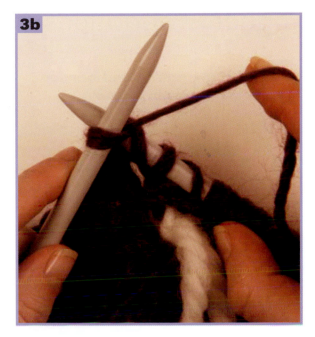

3b

3 K2, m1, K2tog, K1. m1 (this is the place in the row where the increases and decreases take place to make the points). K1, * m1, K2tog * . Repeat from * to* as required. There should be 11 stitches on the needle.

4 Knit back over 6 sts until only 5 sts remain on the needle. P3, K2.

5 Repeat steps **1** to **4** until there are 18 sts on the needle (17 rows, ending with step **1**).

6 Row 18. Cast off 9 sts. Knit the remaining 9 sts (this includes the loop that is already on the needle left over from the casting off) thus: K3 sts, P3 sts, K2 sts.

7 Repeat steps **1** to **6** until you have knitted.

8 Decorate the points and the border with paua shell discs.

Lagoon 2 variations

▶ **Large-scale points and border in ribbon and glitter yarn**

Cast on 9 sts using 8mm (US11) needles in 1 strand Colinette **Giotto** shade Popsicle and 1 strand Texere **Stardust** shade Tango. There are 8 increases worked one at a time on every odd row number 8 times in all for side of the point. Once this stage is completed you will commence casting off these same 8 sts on the next even-numbered row until you are left with 9 sts. This is the same number of sts that you cast on at the start of the pattern. Note that to keep the repeat of the mesh pattern correct every other odd-numbered row ends with a K1 (rows 1, 5 and 9, for example) whilst rows 3, 7 and 11, for example, end with a K2 together.

1 K2, m1, K2tog, K1. m1 (this is the place in the row where the increases and decreases take place to make the points). K1, m1, K2tog, K1. There should be 10 sts on the needle.

2 Knit all 10 stitches.

3 K2, m1, K2tog, K1. m1 (this is the place in the row where the increases and decreases take place to make the points). K1, m1, K2tog, m1, K2tog. There should be 11 sts on the needle.

4 Knit all 11 sts.

5 Repeat steps **1** to **4** until there are 17 sts on the needle (15 rows, ending with step **3**).

6 Row 16. Cast off 8 sts. Knit the remaining 9 sts (this includes the loop which is already on the needle left over from the casting off).

7 Repeat as many times as is required.

▶ Tape yarn and glitter wide border

Knitted over 12 sts in **Enigma** shade Frangipani from Colinette and Texere **Stardust** shade Tango.

1 K2, * m1, K2tog, K1*. Repeat from * to * twice in all. m1 (this is the place in the row where the increases and decreases take place to make the points). K1, m1, K2tog, K1. There should be 13 sts on the needle.

2 Knit all 13 sts.

3 K2, * m1, K2tog, K1*. Repeat from * to * twice in all. m1 (this is the place in the row where the increases and decreases take place to make the points). K1, m1, K2tog, m1, K2tog. There should be 14 sts on the needle.

4 Knit all 14 sts.

5 Repeat steps **1** to **4** until there are 19 sts on the needle (13 rows, ending with step **1**).

6 Row 14. Cast off 7 sts. Knit the remaining 9 sts (this includes the loop which is already on the needle left over from the casting off).

7 Repeat as many times as is required.

◀ Pointed lace border in knit and purl stitches

Cast on 12 sts using 7mm (US 10.5/11) needles and I strand each of Colinette **Giotto** yarn shade Popsicle and 1 strand each of shade Tango in **Stardust** and **Prism** from Texere yarns.

Work as for Sample 3 (above) except that the even-numbered rows are knitted in a knit and purl sequence thus:
Row 2 – K5, P6, K2
Row 4 – K6, P6, K2
Row 6 – K7, P6, K2

Continue to increase in this manner until there are 19 sts on the needle. The back row is knitted thus: cast off 7 sts, K4 (includes 1 st remaining on the needle after the cast off), P6, K2.

Carnival

These wavy openwork stitch patterns are designed so that you end up with exactly the same number of stitches at the beginning and end of each pattern row. For every eyelet, which is essentially an increased stitch, you will need to make an equivalent number of decreases.

To make an eyelet in between two adjacent knit stitches, bring the yarn forward as if to purl before knitting into the next knit stitch, making an additional loop (one extra stitch). This loop is knitted in on the next row.

To compensate for the made stitch, knit two stitches together by inserting the point of the needle between two stitches instead of one and knit them off together.

The placement of the increases and decreases will depend upon the type of stitch pattern, and need not necessarily be adjacent to one another. These wavy stitch patterns cluster groups of increases and decreases together to form the characteristic appearance of this type of design.

To knit the elongated decrease mentioned in *Carnival 1*, insert the needle between 2 stitches as you would to make a normal length decrease, but wrap the yarn around the needles twice, as described in Workshop One, for elongated stitches.

Carnival 1

This fluffy boa is knitted on two needles using a combination of multiple increases and elongated decreases. The stitch pattern is repeated every two rows and is moderately easy to knit.

The finished length of this boa is 78¾in (200cm) approximately.

Materials
- 2 x 50g balls each **A** – Sirdar **Gigi** shade 050 (Parisian Purple) and **B** – Sirdar **Gigi** shade 049, Can-Can Pink
- 2 X 50g balls of **C** – Texere **Stardust** shade Tango
- 2 X 50g hanks **D** – Noro **Blossom** shade 5

Equipment
- 1 pair 6mm (US 10) knitting needles

Techniques
- Cast on and off
- Knit
- Purl
- Made stitches
- Elongated decease, knit 2 together method

Knitting Notes
The yarn combinations are made up of the main colour, which is 1 strand **Gigi** (changing from **A** to **B** at random) plied with 2 strands of yarn **C**, whilst the contrast colour is **D**.

Main colour and contrast colour are exchanged every two rows.

1 Using 6mm (US 10) needles cast on 22sts and K1 row in **A**.

2 Continue knitting in **A**. K2, * K2 together elongated twice **a b c** m1, K1 three times, *repeat from * to * twice. K2 together elongated twice, K2.

3 K2, P18, K2.

4 Continue repeating steps **2** and **3**, exchanging colours as described in Knitting Notes.

5 Knit until yarn runs out or stop at the desired length. Cast off.

Carnival 1 variations

▶ Gold eyelets with fluffy stripes

A is Rowan **Lurex Shimmer** 332, **B** is Sirdar **Gigi** 050, **C** is Sirdar **Gigi** 049, **D** is Noro **Blossom** (all used 2 strand throughout) on 6mm (US 10) needles. **1** Cast on 22sts and knit 1 row in **A**. **2** Continue knitting in **A**. K2, * K2tog twice, m1 K1, 3 times in all, * repeat from * to * twice then K2tog twice, K2. **3** K2 P18 K2. **4** Repeat steps **2** and **3** a total of 6 times. **5** Leaving **A** attached to the knitting change to contrast colour and repeat step **2**. **6** K22. Leave contrast colour attached. **7** Change back to **A**. K2, * m1, K2tog elongated *. Repeat from * to * until 2 sts remain. K2. **8** In **A** K22 sts. **9** Contrast colour, as step **2**. **10** Contrast colour, as step **6**. Break off contrast colour. **11** Repeat steps **2** to **10** alternating the contrast colour, as above, as many times as required. Repeat step **4** once more and cast off.

◀ Stripes and eyelets stitched in contrasting textures

A stripe pattern developed around step **7** of the main pattern. The eyelet pattern is knitted thus. Knit one row in colour **A** (two strands of Texere **Stardust** in shade Tango (20% Lurex and 80% viscose), for the next row repeat step **7**, followed by 2 rows of garter stitch. Knit stripes of stocking stitch in contrasting colours of between 2 and 4 rows to divide the pattern rows from each other.

▶ Wavy stripes in contrasting textures

Here steps **2** and **3** from the main pattern are developed into a simple wavy striped design. Repeat these two steps four times in colour **A** (Carnival 1) followed by one repeat in a contrasting yarn and colour.

◀ Wavy stripes and eyelets combined

A development of Sample 3 (above) into an openwork design that is made up of several repeats of the main stitch pattern but this time with elongated stitches on the decreases (step **2**). This design also incorporates one repeat of the eyelet pattern as described in step **7**. Divide the sections with 2 rows of garter stitch in contrast yarns and colours.

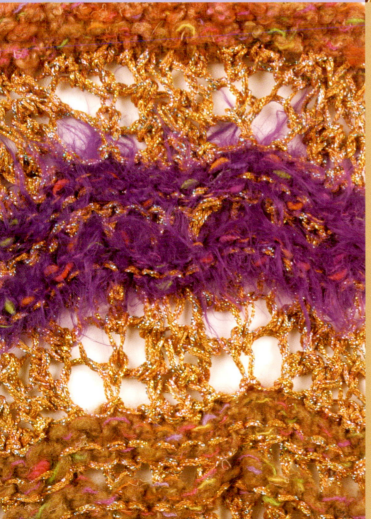

Carnival 2

A heavier-weight boa knitted sideways on a circular needle in contrasting colours and textures, with optional attached pompoms. The knitting is relatively simple. The circular needle is used in the same way as if you were knitting on two needles, but giving you the extra length for the number of stitches cast on.

This boa is approximately 74¾in (190cm) long measured without the pompoms.

Materials
- 1 x 1¾oz (50g) ball each of **A** – Wendy **Shimmer** shade 2048, **C** – Stylecraft **Milan** and **D** – Stylecraft **Mardi Gras** shade 2078 Fiesta.
- 2 x 1¾oz (50g) balls **B** – Stylecraft **Stardust** DK in shade purple/silver mix

Equipment
- 1 pair 9mm (US 13) circular needles used as for straight knitting (see *Carnival 1*, page 146)
- Card template for pompom – cut 2 discs of stout card each 2¾in (7cm) in diameter with a ¾in (2cm) hole in the middle (see page 19)

Techniques
- Cast on and off
- Knit
- Purl
- Made stitches
- Decreased stitches knit 2 together method
- Elongated stitches with 1 extra throw

Knitting Note
Colour **B** is knitted double throughout.

1 Using 9mm (US 13) circular knitting needles and **A** and **B** together cast on 136 stitches and knit 1 row.

2 Change to **C** and knit 1 row elongated stitches.

3 Change to **A** and **B** together and knit 1 row normal length stitches.

4 Change to **B** and **D** together and knit 1 row normal length stitches.

5 Continue knitting in **B** and **D** together and work the main 17 stitch repeat eyelet pattern thus: *K2 together **a** three times in all, M1 **b** K1 **c** five times in all, M1, then K2 together **d** three times in all *. Repeat these instructions 8 times in all.

6 Continue knitting in **B** and **D** together and purl 1 row.

7 Repeat steps **5** and **6** 3 times in total.

8 As step **3**.

9 As step **2**.

10 Repeat step **3** twice in total.

11 Change to **D** and 1 end only of colour **B** and cast off all stitches.

12 Make 6 pompoms in a mix of all the boa colours (see page 19 for instructions). To attach them to the short ends of the boa, cut three ends of yarn per pompom, two each of **D** and one of **B**.

Stitch these three ends through the yarn that is tying the pompom together. Plait together leaving about 4in (10cm) unplaited.

Poke the short ends of the plait yarns through a stitch on the cast-off edge of the boa from front to back. Wrap these ends together with the plait with 2 strands of **B** for 10/12 wraps. Pull the wrapping end through the binding to secure. Trim the yarns to make a mini tassel.

Carnival 2 variations

▶ **Sideways knitted in contrasting textures**

Knitted on 6mm (US 10) needles, this swatch introduces 2 strands of **Gypsy** from Stylecraft in shade 5118 Mystic (colour **E**) into the mix. Cast on 34 stitches in **E** and knit 1 row in **D**. Knit three repeats of the main eyelet pattern as described above in **D**. Knit 2 rows each of **B**, **E** and **B**. Knit three repeats of the main eyelet pattern and 1 further row in **D**. Cast off in **E**.

◀ **Sideways knitted mirror image design**

Cast on 34 stitches with 8mm (US 11) needles in **E**. Change to **B** and knit 1 row. Continue knitting in **B** for 3 repeats of the eyelet pattern as described above. Change to **C** knit 1 row. Knit 2 rows each of **B**, **E** and **B** and 1 row of **C**. The remainder of the sample is a mirror image of the first sections. Use lengthways and decorate with fringing.

153

YARN INDEX

Amelie
100% polyamide nylon.
Ball band tension for 4in (10cm):
11 stitches and 17 rows knitted
on 7–8mm (US 10.5/11) needles.
Approximately 71yd (65m) to
1¾oz (50g).
Shade 03 – *Ice Queen 2*, p88

Bigga by Sirdar
50% acrylic, 50% wool.
Ball band tension for 4in (10cm):
6 stitches and 9 rows knitted on
15mm (US 19) needles.
Approximately 43¾yd (40m) to
3½oz 100g.
Delta Blue (688) – *Cocoon 1*, p57

Biggy Print by Rowan
100% merino wool.
Ball band tension for 4in (10cm):
5.5 stitches and 7 rows knitted
on 20mm (US 35/36) needles.
Approximately 33yd (30m) to
3½oz (100g).
Giddy (239) and Sheep (258) –
Cocoon 2, p64

Blossom by Noro
40% wool, 30% kid mohair, 20%
silk, 10% nylon.
Shade 5 – *Carnival 1*, p145

Enigma by Colinette
55% cotton, 45% rayon.
Ball band tension for 4in (10cm):
14 stitches and 20 rows knitted
on 6mm (US 10) needles.
Approximately 175yd (160m) to
3½oz (100g).
Sahara (135) – *Lagoon 1*, p133,
Jay (85) – *Lagoon 2*, p138

Eskimo by Stylecraft
100% polyester.
Ball band tension for 4in (10cm):
30 rows and 22 stitches square
knitted on 4mm (US 6) needles.
Approximately 98½yd (90m) per
1¾oz (50g).
Kingfisher (5480), Fusion (5482)
and Jade (5483) – *Octopus 2*,
p116

Firecracker from Colinette
Ball band tension for 4in (10cm):
8 stitches and 12 rows knitted on
10mm (US 15) needles.
Approximately 76½yd (70m) to
3½oz (100g).
Magenta – *Reef 2*, p128

Fizz by Sirdar
55% viscose, 19% acrylic,
17% nylon, 9% polyester.
Ball band tension for 4in (10cm):
24 rows and 18 stitches, knitted
on 5mm (US 8) needles.
Approximately 82yd (75m) per
1¾oz (50g).
Fiesta – *Octopus 2*, p116

Gigi by Sirdar
100% nylon.
Ball band tension for 4in (10cm):
25 stitches and 34 rows knitted
on 4mm (US 6) needles.
Approximately 125¾yd (115m)
to 1¾oz (50g).
Electrique Blue (051) –
Allsorts 1, p43,
Etoile Black (046) and Citron
Lime (043) – *Allsorts 2*, p50
Parisian Purple (050) and
Can-can Pink (049) –
Carnival 1, p145

Giotto by Colinette
50% cotton, 40% rayon,
10% nylon.
Ball band tension for 4in (10cm):
11 stitches and 16 rows knitted
on 8mm (US 11) needles.
Approximately 157½yd (144m)
to 3½oz (100g).
Sahara (135) – *Lagoon 1*, p133
and *Relax 2*, p36

Goldfingering by Twilley's
20% metallized polyester,
80% viscose.
WG 62 – *Allsorts 1*, p43

Gypsy by Stylecraft
100% nylon.
Ball band tension for (4in) 10cm:
22 stitches and 34 rows knitted
on 4mm (US 6) needles.
Approximately 67¾yd (62m) to
1¾oz (50g).
Fantasy (5114) – *Allsorts 2*, p50

Icicle by Stylecraft
62% polyester, 38% metallized
polyester.
Ball band tension for 4in (10cm):
22 stitches and 30 rows knitted
on 4mm (US 6) needles.
Approximately 87½yd (80m) to
1¾oz (50g).
Pale pink – *Ice Queen 2*, p88;
White – *Ice Queen 1*, p81

Intension by GGH
100% nylon.
Ball band tension for 4in (10cm):
8 stitches and 13 rows knitted on
10–12mm (US 15–17) needles.
Approximately 87½yd (80m) to
1¾oz (50g).
05 – *Allsorts 1*, page 45

Isis by Colinette
100% viscose.
Ball band tension for 4in (10cm):
11 stitches and 16 rows knitted
on 7mm (US 10.5/11) needles.
Approximately 109⅓yd (100m)
to 3½oz (100g).
Sahara (135) – *Relax 2*, p36;
Morocco (127) – *Relax 1*, p29

Lurex Shimmer by Rowan
80% viscose, 20% polyester.
Ball band tension for 4in (10cm):
29 stitches and 41 rows knitted
on 3.25mm (US 3) needles.
Approximately 104yd (95m) to
¾oz (25g).
Antique White Gold (332) –
Carnival 1, p145

Mardi Gras by Stylecraft
99% acrylic, 1% nylon.
Ball band tension for 4in (10cm):
14 stitches and 20 rows knitted
on 6mm (US 10) needles.
Approximately 102¾yd (94m) to
1¾oz (50g).
Fiesta (2078) –
Carnival 2, p150

Milan by Stylecraft
100% polyester.
Ball band tension for 4in (10cm):
9 stitches and 14 rows knitted on
8mm (US 11) needles.
Approximately 38¼yd (35m) to
1¾in (50g).
Carnival 2, p150

Plume by Elle
100% polyester.
Ball band tension for 4in (10cm):
18 stitches and 26 rows to
square knitted on 4–5mm (US
6/9) needles. Approximately
65½yd (60m) to 1¾oz (50g).
Shade 222 – *Octopus 1*, p109

Prism by Texere
100% viscose rayon
Approximately 284¼yd (260m)
to 3½oz (100g).
Tango – *Lattice 1*, p95;
Peacock – *Lattice 2*, p102

Shimmer by Wendy
100% polyester.
Ball band tension for 4in (10cm):
19 stitches and 729 rows knitted
on 4.5mm (US 7) needles.
Approximately 71yd (65m) to
1¾oz (50g).
2046 – *Reef 1*, p121;
2048 – *Carnival 2*, p150

Shimmer 5 by Colinette
50% viscose, 50% wool.
Ball band tension for 4in (10cm):
7.5 stitches and 10 rows knitted
on 12mm (US 17) needles.
Approximately 52½yd (48m) to
3½oz (100g).
Sahara (135) and Morocco (127)
– *Relax 1*, p31

Silk Garden by Noro
45% silk, 45% kid mohair,
10% lambswool.
213 – *Ripple 2*, p76

Snowdrift by Stylecraft
100% polyester.
Ball band tension for 10cm: 22
stitches and 30 rows knitted on
size 4mm (US 6) needles.
Approximately 98½yd (90m) to
1¾oz (50g).
Pale pink – *Ice Queen 2*, p88

Stardust by Texere
20% lurex and 80% viscose
Approximately 437½yd (400m)
to 3½oz (100g).
Deep mauve – Lagoon 2, p138,
Tango – *Lattice 1*, p95,
Kingfisher – *Lattice 2*, p102

Stardust DK
91% acrylic, 6% polyester,
3% nylon
Ball band tension for 4in (10cm):
20 stitches and 28 rows knitted
on 4mm (US 6) needles.
Approximately 147½yd (135m)
to 1¾oz (50g).
Black/silver – *Allsorts 2*, p50;
Purple/silver – *Carnival 2*, p150

Stars by GGH
86% nylon and 14% polyester
Ball band tension for 4in (10cm):
17 stitches and 21 rows knitted
on 7–8mm (US 10.5/11) needles.
Approximately 142yd (130m) to
1¾oz (50g).
Shade 05 – *Reef 2*, p128

Velvet Touch by Wendy
100% nylon
Ball band tension for 4in (10cm):
19 stitches and 30 rows knitted
on 3.75–4.5mm (US 5–6)
needles. Approximately 115yd
(105m) to 1¾oz (50g).
Rich Turqoise (2054) – *Reef 1*,
p121 and *Allsorts 1*, p43,
Plum (2052) – *Allsorts 1*, p43

Vision ribbon by Texere
100% viscose
Approximately 229½yd (210m)
to 3½oz (100g).
Red – *Reef 2*, page 128

Wow by Sirdar
100% polyester
Ball band tension for 4in (10cm):
8 stitches and 15 rows knitted on
7mm (US 10.5/11) needles.
Approximately 63½yd (58m) to
3½oz (100g).
Blue Ice (751) – *Ripple 1*, p73

155

MAIL ORDER YARNS AND SUPPLIERS

Angel Yarns
Worldwide online shop where some of the more hard to find and interesting hand-knitting yarn can be found including Noro, Elle, GGH (Rebecca).
☎ 0044 (0) 1273 276765
Email knitting@angelyarns.com
Web www.angelyarns.com

Baba Beads
Online supplier of wood, glass, metal beads.
PO Box 505, Walton-On-Thames, Surrey, KT12 3XT, UK.
☎ 07754 981249
Email info@bababeads.com

Colinette Yarns Ltd
UK - Colinette Yarns Ltd, Banwy Workshops, Llanfair, Caereinion, Powys, Wales, SY21 0SG, UK. Shop online, by post or visit their shop (check for opening times).
☎ 01938 810128
Email feedback@colinette.com
Web www.colinette.com
USA - Unique Kolours, 28n. Bacton Hill Road, Malvern, PA 19355, USA

Kangaroo
Worldwide mail order service for a wide range of knitting yarns including Noro.
☎ 01273 814900
Email sales@kangaroo.uk.com
Web www.kangaroo.uk/com

KCG Trading
Knitting and Crochet supplies (including large-sized cable needles) by mail order:
PO Box 145, Leeds, LS8 2WS, UK

☎ 0113 2664651
Email kcgtl2000@hotmail.com
Web www.kcgtrading.com

Ocean Shell Shop
Online suppliers based in New Zealand of paua shell beads and buttons.
Email info@oceanshellnz.co
Web www.oceanshell.com

Patons
Patons fashion yarn (Whisper, Symphony and Glitz).
Web www.coates.co.uk

Thomas B Ramsden & Co (Bradford) Ltd
Suppliers of Wendy Velvet Touch, Wendy Shimmer and Twilleys Goldfingering. UK customers should contact the company to find the nearest retail outlet.
☎ 01943 872264
Email sales@tbramsden.co.uk
Web www.tbramsden.co.uk

Rowan
Internet, high street and mail order supplies UK and world-wide Rowan yarn stockists directory can be viewed on their website.
Rowan Yarns, Green Lane Mill, Holmfirth, West Yorkshire, HD9 2DX, UK.
☎ 01484 681 881
Email mail@knitrowan.com
Web www.knitrowan.com

Sirdar
Suppliers of Sirdar Fizz (revamped after health and safety product recall), Gigi. For

UK and worldwide stockists contact the company.
☎ 01924 371 501
Email enquiries@sirdar.co.uk
Web www.sirdar.co.uk

Streamers
Beads and sequins online.
Unit 1, Tavistock House, Tavistock Street, Bletchley, Milton Keynes, MK22P, UK.
☎ 01908 644411
Email sales@streamers.co.uk
Web www.streamers.co.uk

Stylecraft
Milan, Gypsy, Icicle, Snowdrift, Mardi Gras, Eskimo and many other fashion yarns. Currently the company does not have online ordering facilities. UK customers should contact Stylecraft to find the nearest retail outlet.
Stylecraft, PO Box 62, Goulbourne St, Keighley, West Yorks, BD21 1PP, UK.
☎ 01535 669 952

Texere Yarns
Mail order service and mill shop including Prism viscose and Stardust glitter yarns.
☎ 01274 722191
Email info@texereyarns.co.uk
Web www.texereyarns.co.uk

Yarn Market
Mail order USA includes GGH (Rebecca), Noro, Sirdar, Rowan, Tahki (eyelash yarns), Stacy Charles, Prism Yarns and Crystal Palace yarns.
Web www.yarnmarket.com

ABOUT RUTH LEE

My formal qualifications are in printed textile design. My original ambition in the late 1970s was to set up as a maker in painted and printed textiles, but the cost was too great. At the time I was interested in large-scale installation work and hand painting lengths of fabric. I bought a knitting machine simply to produce saleable items with a view to setting up in print at a later date, having seen one in action by a fellow student on my postgraduate course at Birmingham Polytechnic.

At the time I had never really considered knitting as a potential career. Although I knitted as a child (and was surrounded with and greatly appreciated the beautiful hand-knits that my mum made) I never really had the patience to finish (or even start) projects other than playful and eccentric interpretations of stitch patterns in my mum's pattern books. I do remember knitting a few sweaters in my teenage years and incorporated some free-form knitting into college projects, but I did much more in the way of sewing and artwork.

However, once I had mastered the basics of the knitting machine (I am completely self taught) I quickly became fascinated by all the different types of colourful patterns and textures that could be produced, away from the constraints of a written pattern. Machine-knitting was a much more visual experience (graphs, charts, free form knitting) and suited my way of thinking. I then found I had unlimited patience to produce hand-tooled, machine-knitted fabrics directly on the machine and now take the same approach to hand-knitting.

I am currently exploring hand-knitting within the broad area of my fibre arts practice. I do not differentiate between hand-framed machine-knitting and hand-knitting with needles. It is all about creating continuous loop structures. I use the machine as a

Photo: Cumbrian Newspapers

hand tool in much the same way as I work with hand-knitting needles. My current approach to hand-knitting owes much to my experimental machine knitting, as one working method complements the other.

Latterly I see myself as a fibre artist who knits, rather than knitted textile designer/knitwear designer, seeing each element of my practice (site specific fibre arts work, exhibitions, wire knitted jewellery and accessories, book projects, workshops, writing for knitting magazines) as complementing one another.

My current exhibition work is multi-disciplinary in approach, and explores, for example, continuous loop technique (hand and machine), off-loom construction techniques, surface design and manipulation.

INDEX

ACKNOWLEDGMENTS

Ruth Lee would like to thank the following:

Rowan Yarns and in particular Ann Hinchcliffe for all those last minute requests especially the yarn for the step by step guides.

Colinette at Colinette Yarns

John Frankish and Gill Penny-Larter at Stylecraft

Tony Robinson at Thomas B. Ramsden

Pauline Brown at Sirdar

Tracy Whittington at Patons UK

Robin Smith at Texere Yarns

Angel Yarns

Baba Beads

Streamers

GMC Publications Limited would like to thank the following:

Aline Tanner and Rose Marshall for modelling the boas and scarves.

Virginia Brehaut, Tracy Hallett, Andrew Humm and Gilda Pacitti for lending props for photography.

To request a catalogue or place an order for Guild of Master Craftsman titles, please contact:

GMC Publications, Castle Place, 166 High Street, Lewes, East Sussex BN7 1XU, United Kingdom Tel: 01273 488005 Fax: 01273 402866

www.gmcbooks.com